THE KNITTER'S BIBLE

knitted
afghans & pillows

THE KNITTER'S BIBLE

knitted
afghans and pillows

CLAIRE CROMPTON

D&C
David and Charles
www.mycraftivity.com

A DAVID & CHARLES BOOK
Copyright © David & Charles Limited 2008

David & Charles is an F+W Publications Inc. company
4700 East Galbraith Road
Cincinnati, OH 45236

First published in the UK and US in 2008

Text and designs copyright © Claire Crompton 2008
Photography, illustrations and layout copyright © David & Charles 2008

A catalogue record for this book is available from the British Library.

ISBN-13: 978-0-7153-2738-8 paperback
ISBN-10: 0-7153-2738-0 paperback

Printed in China by SNP Leefung
for David & Charles
Brunel House   Newton Abbot   Devon

Commissioning Editor: Jennifer Fox-Proverbs
Desk Editor: Bethany Dymond
Project Editor: Nicola Hodgson
Art Editors: Sarah Underhill and Charly Bailey
Designer: Emma Sandquest
Production Controller: Kelly Smith
Photographer: Lorna Yabsley

Visit our website at www.davidandcharles.co.uk

David & Charles books are available from all good bookshops; alternatively you
can contact our Orderline on 0870 9908222 or write to us at FREEPOST EX2 110,
D&C Direct, Newton Abbot, TQ12 4ZZ (no stamp required UK only); US customers
call 800-289-0963 and Canadian customers call 800-840-5220.

contents

beautify your home!

Knitting for your home is a lovely way to add a touch of handmade beauty to your interiors. You can dress your furniture with knitted throws and cushions – add seasonal colour by working the projects in strong, bright shades for spring and summer and warm, rich shades for autumn and winter. Add drama for a party by draping a beaded throw, introduce fleeting fashion shades without having to repaint your walls, or add a single focal point of colour to a minimalist white interior. Knitted items are also a fantastic way to introduce colour and texture into your home, matching or contrasting with your colour scheme.

Most of the projects in this book are for people with a basic knowledge of knitting. Some projects, such as the Spring Greens basic cushions (pages 24–29) and On the Fringes, a basic garter stitch throw (pages 20–23), are designed to encourage beginners to have a go at knitting for the home. But there are plenty of projects for experienced knitters too; Hedgerow Harlequin, a mitred square throw (pages 50–53), and the Rustic Entrelac throw (pages 66–73) show how two methods of patchwork knitting can be used to make large-scale pieces of knitted fabric. Cables are used for the Celtic Knot Garden floor cushion (pages 36–39) and French knitting is given a new twist for two sizes of cushion (French Fancies; pages 74–79). Intarsia is used for the Wobbly Stripe seat (pages 92–95), while lace knitting features in the Romantic Roses bedspread and pillowcase (pages 86–91).

Use thick yarns and big needles for large-scale impact such as the Life's a Beach throw and cushion (pages 62–65), or take a little more time to produce closely worked fabric such as the

Denim Delight textured throw (pages 80–85). Many of the projects are knitted in panels so you don't have too many stitches on your needles at any one time. Doing this also makes it easier to adjust the size of the item; just add more panels for a larger throw or work fewer panels and use the piece as a wall hanging or as a rug. The Rose Garden bedspread (pages 86–89) could easily be made bigger for a larger bed, while the Rippling Waves throw (pages 96–99) would look stunning as a wall hanging three or four panels wide.

For each project I have given ideas for using different yarns and colours so you can incorporate the knitted pieces into your interior colour scheme. Yarn Focus is an explanation of why I chose the yarn that I have used, while Design Secrets Unravelled suggests yarns and colours to give the projects a different twist. I've also used mixed media combined with yarn; the Mixing It Up table runner and cushion (pages 44–49) show the impact of using braids, ribbons and furnishing trims to add texture to a simple garter-stitch piece. These can also be used to trim a simple knitted piece; beads and sequins can be added, such as on the Terrific Trimmings beaded throw and cushion (pages 30–35), for extra flair.

All the techniques that are used to make the projects in this book are explained in detail in the resource section (pages 103–123), which also contains clear diagrams and reference to the projects. Should you want to recreate the projects exactly as they appear in the book, there is a list of the yarns used (pages 124–126) and a comprehensive list of suppliers (page 127).

So, take your needles and start beautifying your home today!

in the beginning...

fibres

For the projects in this book, I have considered whether they need to be made of tough fibres to resist wear, such as cotton or wool, or are suitable to be worked in softer fibres, such as silk, because they are more decorative than practical. For example, a throw draped over a bed will get less wear and tear than one covering a sofa, while a floor cushion or seating cube needs to be made of more robust yarn than cushions scattered on an armchair.

The guide to natural and synthetic fibres below will help you think about the textures, finish and weight of the various yarns available. Think carefully about what type of yarn would be most suitable for your home furnishing project. Some fibres, such as angora or mohair, shed hairs, so these are not practical yarns to make an everyday throw covering a sofa – just think of all those hairs getting on your clothes! However, these are great fibres to use to make soft, fluffy bedroom throws and cushions. Some yarns combine more fragile fibres with more robust ones; silk mixed with wool, for example, produces a fabric with the sheen of the silk but with the hard-wearing qualities of the wool. Some fibres cost more than others; throws take up a large quantity of yarn, so you could keep expensive fibres for smaller cushions or combine them in stripes or blocks with less costly yarns.

NATURAL FIBRES

Alpaca is spun from the coat of the alpaca, a close relation of the llama. It is a wonderfully soft and lustrous yarn, which has many of the qualities of cashmere but at a more affordable price. Angora yarn can shed hairs, so it may be unsuitable for high-use items.

Angora hair comes from the angora rabbit. A yarn with a high content of angora is very fluffy and sheds hairs. It is usually blended with another fibre to give it stability, making a super-soft yarn ideal for feminine cushions.

Cashmere is spun from the hair of the cashmere goat. Pure cashmere yarn is very expensive and best kept for luxurious cushions. When it is blended with another fibre such as wool it becomes much more affordable.

Cotton comes from the ball of the cotton plant. It is a heavy fibre, very hard-wearing, and available in a great range of colours. Cotton can be mercerized; this is a process to give it lustre and take brighter dyes. Matte cotton tends to be more loosely spun. Use it for bright summer throws or floor cushions.

Linen comes from the stem of the flax plant, and it is often blended with cotton to soften it. In its natural colour, it will add rustic simplicity to a country cottage; dyed and it has an understated elegance, ideal for city chic.

Mohair is spun from the coat of the angora goat. The softer kid mohair is the first or second shearing of a kid goat and is finer than the mohair from the adult goat. Mohair is usually blended with another fibre to give it strength. It is light and so is ideal for soft, cosy bedroom throws.

Silk is a continuous filament secreted by the silkworm larva, which it spins around itself to form a cocoon. This cocoon is unwound and many of these fibres are spun together to form a yarn. Silk has a lustre, is soft, and has a dry feel. Use it blended with cotton or wool to make it more hard-wearing. It adds luxury to any room.

Wool is spun from the fleece of a sheep; different breeds of sheep give different qualities of yarn. Merino wool is very soft, Shetland is more hard-wearing, Wensleydale is very lustrous and Jacob wool is spun in fantastic natural colours. Wool has excellent insulating qualities; it is warm in winter and cool in summer. Many of the projects in this book use wool and it is a great yarn for a beginner to use. It knits up beautifully and can be pulled back and recycled without loss of quality. Tweed wool adds instant warmth to a room, and natural shades of wool will soften hard urban edges.

BLENDED AND SYNTHETIC FIBRES

Blended yarns of natural and synthetic fibres combine the natural yarn's qualities with the hard-wearing and stable features of the synthetic. Some of the synthetic fibres used in the projects are acrylic, metallic, nylon, polyamide fibre, polyester and viscose. Synthetic fibres are spun into the most wonderful fancy yarns, such as eyelash and ribbon. They take dyes well and will add a vibrant glow of colour to a minimalist interior or clash wonderfully in a retro-inspired room.

FIBRE CHECKLIST
When you are choosing yarn for a knitted project for an interior, use the checklist below to see what qualities your yarn offers.

Hard-wearing: Blended and synthetic fibres, cotton, linen, wool
Luxury: Cashmere, silk
Soft and snuggly: Alpaca, angora, mohair

weight

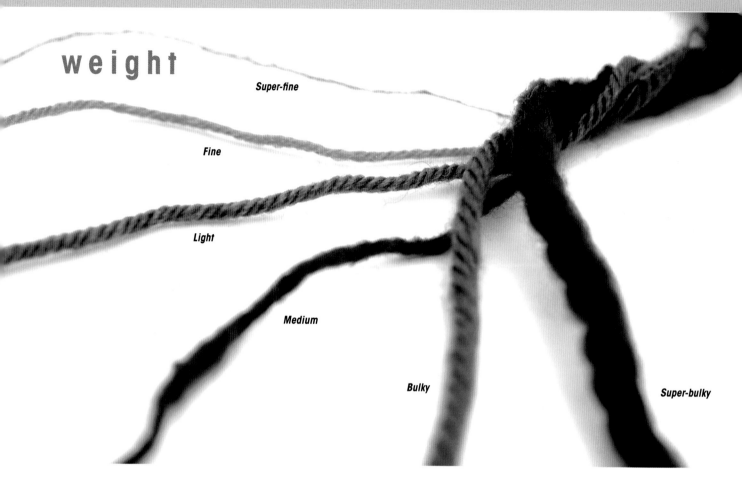

Super-fine

Fine

Light

Medium

Bulky

Super-bulky

The weight of a yarn refers to its thickness; a light-weight yarn is thin, and knits up into a soft, delicate fabric. A medium-weight yarn is thicker and knits up into a chunkier fabric. Experiment with new yarns and discover how a fabric can be changed by altering the weight of yarn used. Thick yarns such as bulky and super-bulky are ideal for knitting up into larger projects such as the Rustic Entrelac throw (pages 66–73). They grow quickly and produce a warm, thick fabric. Light- and medium-weight yarns can be used for finer details on cushions, or for mixing together as in the On the Fringes throw (pages 20–23). Use several strands together of very thin yarns like super-fine weight to make a thicker yarn or add them into a yarn mix.

STANDARD YARN WEIGHTS

weight	gauge*	needle size**	yarn type***
super-fine	27–32 sts	1 to 3 (2.25–3.25mm)	sock, fingering (2ply, 3ply)
fine	23–26 sts	3 to 5 (3.25–3.75mm)	sport, baby (4ply)
light	21–24 sts	5 to 7 (3.75–4.5mm)	light worsted, DK (DK)
medium	16–20 sts	7 to 9 (4.5–5.5mm)	worsted, afghan (aran)
bulky	12–15 sts	9 to 11 (5.5–8mm)	chunky
super-bulky	6–11 sts	11 (8mm) and above	super-chunky

Notes: * Gauge (tension) is measured over 4in/10cm in stockinette (stocking) stitch
** US needle sizes are given first, with UK equivalents in brackets
*** Alternative US yarn type names are given first, with UK equivalents in brackets

YARN WEIGHTS

A light-weight (DK) yarn knits up into a thinner fabric than a medium-weight (aran) yarn. Many of the projects in this book use medium (aran), bulky (chunky) or super-bulky (super-chunky) weight yarns; often several strands of fine (4ply) or light-weight (DK) yarns are used together to make a thicker yarn.

Yarns are sometimes described by a number of ply, for example, 2ply, 4ply or 6ply. A ply is a single twisted strand. As a general rule, the more plies that are twisted together, the thicker the yarn. However, just to confuse things, plies can be different thicknesses themselves. A tightly spun ply will be thinner than a loosely spun one. For example, a 2ply Shetland wool yarn knits up to fine-weight (4ply) gauge, and a thick Lopi yarn (a type of wool traditionally sourced from Iceland) is a single ply.

CRAFT YARN COUNCIL OF AMERICA'S STANDARD YARN WEIGHTS

To avoid confusion when referring to weights of yarn in this book, I have adopted a standard developed by the Craft Yarn Council of America (see table, left), which divides yarns into weight rather than number of plies. Throughout this book I have given a generic description of each yarn used, specifying the weight and type of yarn that I have used for each project. This means that you can use any yarn that is the same weight to knit your project; this is especially useful if the one featured has been discontinued, as happens occasionally. (If you want to use exactly the same yarns for the projects that are featured in this book, see pages 124–126 for details.)

Yarn manufacturers in the US and in the UK sometimes use different names to identify the same weight of yarn. Where they differ, I have included both in the table left. Throughout this book, I give the US weight first, with the UK equivalent following in brackets.

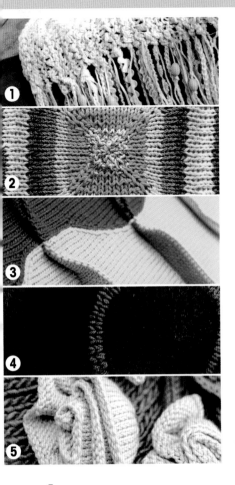

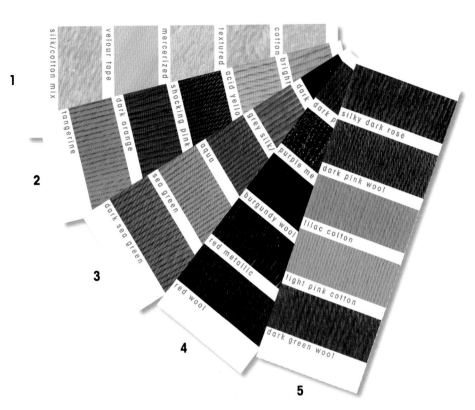

The swatch cards (left to right) are labelled: silk/cotton mix, tangerine, velour tape, dark orange, mercerized, shocking pink, textured, acid yellow, grey silk/, aqua, cotton bright, dark dark p, purple me, silky dark rose, sea green, burgundy wool, dark pink wool, dark sea green, red metallic, lilac cotton, red wool, light pink cotton, dark green wool

colour

Colour is a personal choice; no doubt you have your own favourite palette of colours that you use to create your interior spaces. You may also be inspired by the age or location of your home – modern or period, urban or rural. Below is an introduction to some of the palettes that I have used for the projects in this book, together with some alternative ideas.

A GUIDE TO COLOUR

The palettes described here refer to the colour swatch cards shown above.

Natural palette (1) This palette is calm, restful and sophisticated. It is suitable for a home full of natural materials such as wood, stone and terracotta. These are the colours of nature, including earth pigments like ochre and sand, browns inspired by woodlands, and chocolate and coffee. Shades of grey are inspired by pebbles and stones, while undyed ecru and unbleached linen add an organic tone. The Mixed Messages table runner (pages 44–47) uses a palette of shades of ecru in natural fibres.

Warm palette (2) Warm colours are mixed with red or yellow, so think of orange, orange-yellow, red and hot pink. These shades are fiery, strong and bright, and bring warmth into the home during autumn and winter or add strong colour into a minimalist room. Use shades of red together or mix up shades of spicy orange and yellow-orange. The On the Fringes throw (pages 20–23) uses a warm palette of orange and pink, while the Citrus Squares seating cube (pages 56–59) combines citrus shades of lemon, orange and lime with hot pink.

Cool palette (3) Cool colours are based on blue and yellow, so include green, blue and blue-violet as well as mixes of these shades, such as yellow-green, blue-green, turquoise and purple. These colours are ideal for spring and summer or for light airy rooms such as those decorated in greyed Scandinavian colours. Use shades of one colour; choose sea-inspired blues including aqua, grey-blue and pale turquoise, or shades of green from mint to sage. The Rippling Waves throw (pages 96–99) is worked in cool shades of grey, aqua and blue with flashes of sea greens. The Taking the Floor cushion (page 78) has a cool palette of greens combined with shades of mauve.

Rich palette (4) To add luxury and opulence to a room, think of jewel colours such as ruby, amethyst and emerald. These add drama and mystery and could be used just for the evening or for the Christmas party season. The Sizzling Stripes cushions (pages 40–43) combine shades of red or purple with metallics to create a luxurious look. The Sequinned Shimmer throw (pages 30–33) is a deep purple set off with opulent gold trimmings.

Light palette (5) Light palettes are ideal for spring days, soft feminine bedrooms or country cottages. They include icy pastels like aqua, mint green, peach and pale pink, and soft pastels such as lilac, sugared pink and mauve. The Rose Garden bedspread (pages 86–89) uses a dark rose together with pale pastel rose shades.

11

① ② ③ ④

texture

Yarns are made in a wide range of textures, from plain, plied yarns to extravagant concoctions of ribbon, bouclé or eyelash. Combining different textures together produces fantastic knitted fabrics, such as the On the Fringes throw (pages 20–23) or the Colour Carnival cushion (pages 48–49). Try mixing an eyelash yarn with tweed, or chenille with a metallic thread to make thicker yarns. Keep the textured yarns for plain stitches such as stockinette stitch or garter stitch; stitch patterns and cables are often lost in such yarns. Choose crisp cottons or smooth wools to show off the more complex stitches instead. Use the guide to texture set out here for more information.

Funky loops (1)

Astrakhan yarn has a texture of loose loops that curl across the surface of the fabric. Use a simple stockinette stitch to display its texture fully.

Bouclé has a similar looped texture to astrakhan, formed when a loosely spun strand is allowed to wrap around itself into snarls and snags. Cotton bouclé is crisp and produces a dense texture rather like a towel. Softer bouclés in mohair and wool make a luxurious, deep fabric.

Rich velvet (2)

Chenille is a short-pile yarn that produces a wonderfully thick, velvety fabric. It is available in different weights from fine (4ply) to bulky (chunky). The thicker version would be great on its own; a thinner chenille would add a touch of softness and luxury to a yarn mix.

Modern edge (3)

Metallic yarns are crunchy, futuristic and full of light. They are often a mix of viscose and metallic elements and add a sharp highlight in a soft, fluid fabric. Add these yarns to any yarn mix to create instant glamour.

6   7   8

Mercerized cotton is a tight, lustrous yarn that makes a very clean, crisp fabric. Mercerized cotton contributes one of the vivid reds of the Brilliant Bolster (pages 40–42).

Cord is a smooth, round yarn. When cord is knitted, each stitch sits apart from its neighbours, producing an open fabric. This would add structure to a softer yarn mix.

Fluid (4)

Ribbons can be multi-coloured, stranded with metallic, open or solid structures, fluffy or crisp, slinky or hard. They are flat and vary in width from narrow to wide, and are available in any fibre, from wool to modern synthetics. The Bead Me Up cushion (pages 34–35) uses a bright glossy ribbon yarn for a contemporary feel, while the On the Fringes throw (pages 20–23) features a spicy metallic ribbon in the mix.

Tape is a fluid knitted flat yarn that rarely produces a completely flat fabric; it twists and folds on your needles. It folds in half for one stitch and then opens out for the next. Viscose tapes produce wonderfully slinky fabric.

Fluffy and furry (5)

Mohair is a soft, fluffy yarn; the fibres trap air and light to produce a feather-soft fabric. Use in a mix with heavier yarns to add a haze of colour.

Eyelash yarn looks like a frayed ribbon. Available in width from narrow to outrageously wide, it knits up into a fabric of deep shimmering waves. Try showing it off by working it in stripes with contrasting smooth yarns.

Fake or faux fur produces a deep pile great for winter throws or as a trim around a cushion.

Warm and woolly (6)

Tweed wool yarn is a combination of two or more colours, spun together or introduced as slubs or knots of colour. A knitted tweed fabric looks warm, cosy and resilient. You can contrast it with metallic or cotton for an exciting twist. Pure wool tweed makes fantastic fulled fabric; the colours merge into a dense brushed fabric, as seen on the Celtic Knot Garden cushion (pages 36–39).

Smooth wool yarn shows stitch textures beautifully and is available in a great range of colours. It is

hard-wearing and very easy to knit with. Undyed wool in natural colours can add warmth and a homespun feel to urban interiors.

Dry summer (7)

Matte cotton has a fantastic dry texture; it has weight and will add strength and structure to a yarn mix. The colours can be fantastically dusty, like painted plaster, or zingy like citrus fruit, such as those used in the Citrus Squares seating cube (pages 56–59).

Mixed media (8)

The Mixing It Up runner and cushion (pages 44–49) show how using fibres other than knitting yarn can add unexpected texture. Use ribbons, braids, furnishing trims, strung sequins and beads, or cut fabric and net into strips.

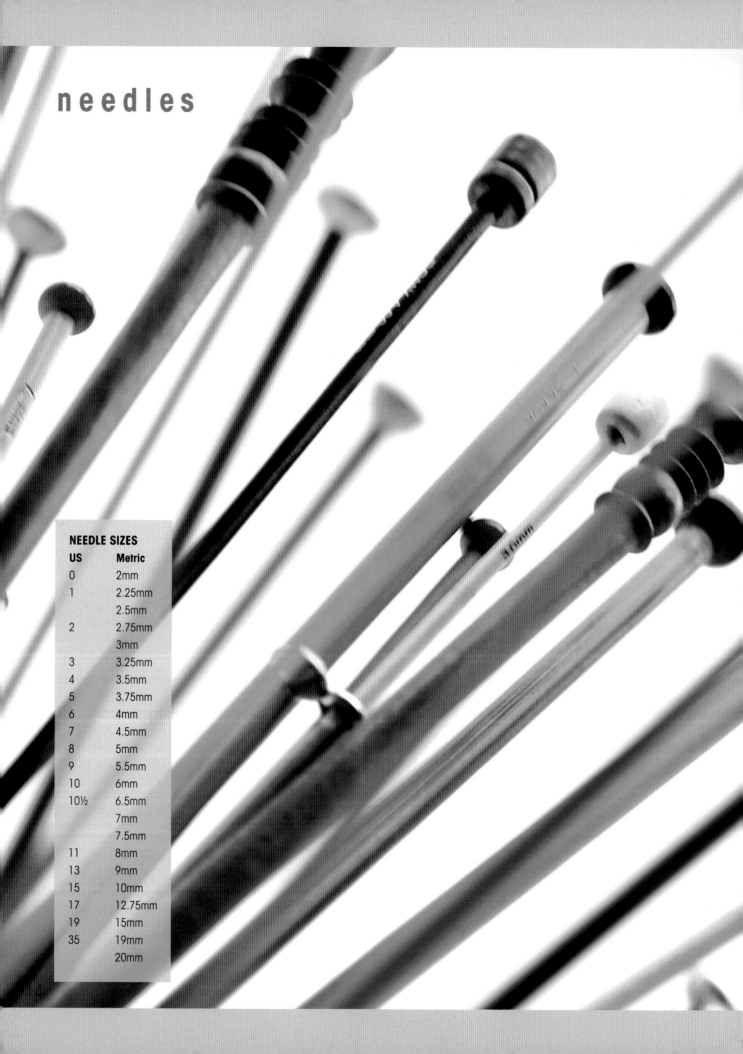

needles

NEEDLE SIZES

US	Metric
0	2mm
1	2.25mm
	2.5mm
2	2.75mm
	3mm
3	3.25mm
4	3.5mm
5	3.75mm
6	4mm
7	4.5mm
8	5mm
9	5.5mm
10	6mm
10½	6.5mm
	7mm
	7.5mm
11	8mm
13	9mm
15	10mm
17	12.75mm
19	15mm
35	19mm
	20mm

needles

gauge

At the beginning of every project, I have given the gauge (tension) that you need to achieve to make the project successfully. The gauge is the number of stitches and rows you need to make a 1in (2.5cm) square. This is a very important part of knitting; if you do not obtain the correct gauge, the throw or cushion may come out bigger or smaller than you would like. It is especially important when you are knitting a cushion to fit a specific size of cushion pad.

GAUGE MEASUREMENTS

The gauge is given over 4in (10cm). For example: the gauge for a light-weight (DK) yarn is 22 stitches and 28 rows to 4in (10cm) measured over stockinette stitch on size 6 (4mm) needles. To check your gauge, you must work a square of fabric measuring at least 6in (15cm), using the stated yarn, needle size and stitch. You can then measure the fabric in the middle of the square, avoiding the edge stitches, which will be distorted.

Sometimes you will find that it is difficult to achieve both the correct stitch and row count for your gauge square. It is usually more important to obtain the correct stitch count, so you should concentrate on achieving that. The row count matters only in projects that are written row by row rather than measured to length, such as the Celtic Knot Garden cushion (pages 36–39).

KNITTING A GAUGE SQUARE

To knit a gauge square in stockinette stitch, you need to cast on the number of stitches stated for 4in (10cm) plus half as many again. For example: 22 sts plus 11 sts.

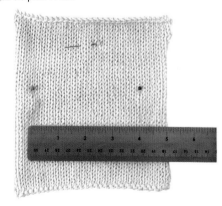

1 Work in stockinette stitch for 6in (15cm) and then bind off loosely.
2 Steam or wet press the square in the way that you will use for your finished project (see page 116). The information on the ball band will tell you whether you can steam the yarn or not.

3 Lay the square on a flat surface without stretching it. Place a ruler horizontally on the square and place a pin 1in (2.5cm) in from the edge and place another at 4in (10cm) from the first pin.
4 Do the same for the rows by placing the ruler vertically, keeping away from the cast-on and bound-off edges, which may pull the fabric in.
5 Count the number of stitches and rows between the pins: this is your gauge. If you have more stitches than the suggested number, your stitches are too small; you will need to use a size larger needle to make the stitches bigger and so obtain fewer stitches to 4in (10cm). If you have too few stitches, this means your stitches are too big; you need to use a size smaller needle to make the stitches smaller and so obtain more to 4in (10cm).
6 Work another square until you achieve the gauge stated in the pattern.

MEASURING TEXTURED YARNS

If you are using a textured yarn, it can be difficult to see individual stitches and rows. For yarns with a long pile, such as the faux fur shown, measure the 4in (10cm) for stitches and rows, placing a marker in a contrasting yarn. Leave long ends on these markers so they are visible through the long pile. Hold the square up to a window or a light (protect your eyes against a strong light). This will show up the stitches and rows clearly for you to count.

With yarns that are heavily textured, such as the bouclé shown, or a thick fleece or plush yarn, the stitches close up and make a uniform surface when knitted. Knit a contrasting coloured sewing cotton in with the yarn. This will show up the stitches and rows and make counting easier. Mark the 4in (10cm) for stitches and rows with a contrasting thread, so you can pull the fabric to make out difficult stitches without losing any pins.

It is often easier to make out the stitches and rows on the wrong side of the square (that is, on the reverse stockinette side), so try using this side to measure over.

If you are not sure what the individual stitches and rows look like, refer to page 105.

MEASURING OVER A STITCH PATTERN

If the gauge is quoted over a stitch pattern like that used for the Denim Delight throw (see pages 80–85), cast on enough stitches to work complete repeats. The repeat of the pattern follows the asterisk; cast on a multiple of this number of stitches plus any stitches given at the beginning and end of the row.

USING GAUGE FOR SUBSTITUTING YARNS

For all these projects, I have suggested other yarns to use or different weights of yarn to mix up into a unique yarn. It is very important to keep aiming for the stated gauge when you alter the yarn mix, or the project will not be the correct size and the finished fabric may be too loose or too tight.

abbreviations

Abbreviations are used in knitting patterns to shorten commonly used terms so that the instructions are easier to read and a manageable length. The following is a list of all the abbreviations you need to make the projects in this book.

alt	alternate
approx	approximately
beg	begin/beginning
cm	centimetre(s)
cont	continue
dec(s)	decrease(s)/decreasing
DK	double knitting
foll	following
g	gram
g st	garter stitch (k every row)
in(s)	inch(es)
inc(s)	increase(s)/increasing
k	knit
k2tog	knit 2 stitches together (decrease 1 stitch)
k3tog	knit 3 stitches together (decrease 2 stitches)
LH	left hand
m	metre(s)
mm	millimetre(s)
M1	make one (increase 1 stitch)
MB	make a bobble
oz	ounces
p	purl
patt(s)	pattern(s)
patt rep(s)	pattern repeat(s)
p2tog	purl 2 stitches together (decrease 1 stitch)
p3tog	purl 3 stitches together (decrease 2 stitches)
psso	pass slipped stitch over
rem	remain/ing
rep(s)	repeat(s)

rev st st	reverse stockinette stitch (1 row p, 1 row k)
RH	right hand
RS	right side
sk2po	slip 1 stitch, knit 2 stitches together, pass slipped stitch over (decrease 2 stitches)
sl	slip
ssk	slip 2 stitches one at a time, knit 2 slipped stitches together (decrease 1 stitch)
ssp	slip 2 stitches one at a time, purl 2 slipped stitches together through the back of the loops (decrease 1 stitch)
st(s)	stitch(es)
st st	stockinette stitch (1 row k, 1 row p) (UK: stocking stitch)
tog	together
WS	wrong side
wyib	with yarn in back
wyif	with yarn in front
yd(s)	yard(s)
yfwd	yarn forward
yo	yarn over
*	repeat directions following * as many times as indicated or until end of row
( )	repeat instructions in round brackets the number of times

In the instructions for the projects, I have favoured US knitting terms. Refer to this box for the UK equivalent.

US TERM	UK TERM
bind off	cast off
gauge	tension
stockinette stitch	stocking stitch
reverse stockinette stitch	reverse stocking stitch
seed stitch	moss stitch
moss stitch	double moss stitch

reading knitting patterns

A knitting pattern tells you how to knit and make up a knitted project. The instructions use shorthand phrases and abbreviations, otherwise they would be far too long. The abbreviations used in this book appear in a list on page 16 with an explanation of what they mean. Many are commonly used, such as k and p. Others refer to special stitches, like C4F. These are explained in the pattern and in the technique section at the back (see page 111 for cables).

WORKING FROM CHARTS

The Wobbly Stripe Seat (pages 92–95) is worked from a colour chart. There are usually very few written instructions for such charts, apart from how many stitches you need to cast on and any knitting that is not included on the chart. Working from charts is explained along with the technique for intarsia on pages 112–113. Sometimes the chart shows any shaping that has to be done, and this will be included in the instructions to set the chart. For example:

Working RS rows (odd) from right to left and WS rows (even) from left to right, and dec 1 st at each end of 13th and every foll 8th row, work in st st from chart until the 64th row has been completed. 52 sts.

IMPERIAL AND METRIC MEASUREMENTS

The patterns are written in both imperial (inches and ounces) and metric (centimetres and grams) measurements, and you should stick to one or the other; some imperial to metric measurements are not exact conversions.

COMMON SHORTHAND PHRASES

You will see some common shorthand phrases appearing in the pattern instructions. These include the following:

cont as set Instead of repeating the same instructions over and over, you must continue to work as previously told.

work as given for To avoid repeating instructions; can be used within one set of instructions or to show how to work another version of the throw or cushion.

* Repeat the directions following * as many times as indicated or until end of row.

** Usually appears at the beginning or beginning and end of a section of instructions and indicates that several rows of instructions should be repeated.

( ) Repeat instructions in round brackets the number of times indicated.

The bold colours and sinuous wavy shapes of the Wobbly Stripe Seat (pages 92–95) are worked using the intarsia method from a chart. See left for more information on working from charts.

and now
to knit…

on the fringes

This wonderfully colourful throw is full of texture, contrasts and variety. Its construction is actually very simple; it is knitted purely in garter stitch, so this is a project that even a beginner could tackle with very satisfying results. The secret to this throw's stupendous style lies in the huge range of yarns used to make it – no fewer than 36 different shades are used, in a variety of weights, fibres and textures. The harmony of the throw lies in the fact that a basic colour palette of pinks and oranges is used throughout. The throw is self-fringing to show off the glorious miscellany of yarns and to add a stylish finish.

The truly unique construction of this throw results in a beautiful range of colour combinations and textures.

DESIGN SECRETS UNRAVELLED...

There is no end to the types of yarns you could use for this throw; it is ideal for using up the yarn left over from another project, oddments or single balls, as well as recycled yarn, bargain-bin finds and swaps. Keep to two ranges of colours as I have; you could use soft pastels instead of strong colours, rich autumnal shades of bronzes and greens, or jewel colours for a luxurious look.

YARN FOCUS

I collected together 18 shades of pink, ranging from pale pink through to hot pink and deep rose-red, and the same number of shades of orange, from pale tangerine to spicy orange, and warm yellow and gold. The texture was just as important as the colour, so among the yarns I have used are fine-weight (4ply) mercerized cottons, light-weight (DK) matte cottons, all weights of smooth wools, eyelash and ladder yarns, brushed 'fleece' yarns, and thick-and-thin, bouclé, ribbon and chenille yarns. Because two yarns are held together to knit each row, thin yarns can be combined with thicker yarns to obtain the correct gauge.

sunset blend

variegated tape

orange fleece

rose pink bouclé

glitter ribbon

bright pink tweed

gold cotton

lipstick cotton

hot pink chenille

bright pink eyelash

on the fringes

This throw is simply constructed in garter stitch; every row is knitted. The fringe is made as you work by leaving long tails of yarn at the beginning and end of each row. The colours are mixed together by using two yarns in each row, so the colour choices are fascinatingly random and anarchic. This is a fun and stimulating way to work, as you never know what you'll end up with!

MEASUREMENTS
59in wide by 79in long (150 by 200cm)

GATHER TOGETHER...
Materials
A 18 mixed yarns of various textures and weights in a range of pink shades, from pale pink to hot pink and light rose to deep rose

B 18 mixed yarns of various textures and weights in a range of oranges, from light orange to spicy orange and lemon yellow to rich golden yellow

Needles
1 size 10½ (7.5mm) 40in (100cm)-long circular needle

GAUGE
12 sts and 24 rows (average) to 4in (10cm) square measured over g st (k every row) using size 10½ (7.5mm) circular needle and one each of yarn A and yarn B

Knit Note: One yarn A and one yarn B are used together throughout. Make sure that you work through both strands for each stitch.

Knit Note: The circular needle is used to accommodate the large number of sts, not for circular knitting. Turn work after every row.

Prepare your project...
Put all the yarns into one bag. Pull out one yarn A and one yarn B at random and start knitting. When you have finished with them, put them both into a second bag. Pull out the next two at random from the first bag and repeat until all the yarns have been used, then begin again. This makes your colour choices totally random and creates some very interesting yarn combinations. If you run out of one yarn, simply replace it with a new one so that you keep 18 of each colour range.

Knit your throw...
Using size 10½ (7.5mm) circular needle and one each of yarn A and yarn B, cast on 165 sts loosely using the cable cast-on method (see page 103), leaving a tail of at least 8in (20cm) at the beginning. Cut off these two yarns, leaving a long tail of a similar length.

Row 1 Join in the next two yarns (one yarn A and one yarn B), leaving a tail of approx 8in (20cm), knit to end. Knot yarn A to yarn B from the row below at both ends of this row.

Rep this row until throw measures 79in (200cm) long.

Bind off, using another set of yarns and leaving long tails at each end of the row. Knot the yarns as before to secure the ends.

to finish...
Pin out to finished measurements and press according to instructions on ball bands.

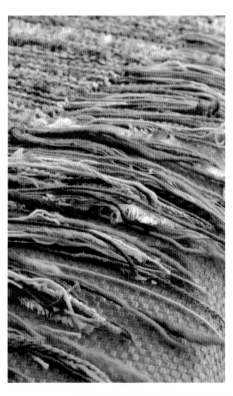

I've suggested leaving a long tail of approximately 8in (20cm) at the end of each row. Use this as a guide only. I didn't measure each time and the fringe is much more interesting for being different lengths.

your yarn, your style!

As a variation, you could work the throw in one range of colours like the blue version shown below; here I have collected together shades of blue in many different textures. This throw still features a fabulous variety of colours and textures within the single-colour theme. The second sample shown here is worked in the complementary colours of purple and green. I've used 18 yarns from each colour range, but you could use more or fewer depending on your personal taste and on the selection of yarns that you can source.

IN THE MIX

A Includes velour tape, mercerized cotton, bouclé and wool tweed, all in shades of light blue, grey-blue and aqua
B Includes silk, bamboo, wool, fleece, lopi wool and cotton denim, all in shades of dark blue, violet-blue and navy

IN THE MIX

A Includes silk/cotton mix, bamboo, metallic, mohair and chenille in shades of purple, lilac and mauve
B Includes matte cotton, wool tweed, alpaca, wool crepe and eyelash in shades of fresh green, leaf green and lime green

spring greens

This project shows you how you can take a basic cushion pattern and give it any number of imaginative variations and embellishments through the addition of trimmings. I've given you four different ideas to alter the basic cushion, ranging from simply sewing on bought trims to making your own pompoms and knitted roses to transform the design. The beauty of working in this way is that you can add as many or as few trimmings as you like, according to your style – go minimalist and just add a simple ribbon for a graceful touch, or go wild and add a mass of extravagant flourishes.

The yarn used for this boudoir-fabulous cushion is a knitted cord in a great olive green that picks up one of the shades in the funky ostrich-feather trim. See page 26.

This elegant cushion is knitted in a textural viscose/silk/linen mix yarn that features multi-coloured threads speckled throughout the fabric. I've decorated this with beaded and sequinned trims in complementary shades of green, using a soft velvet ribbon for a luxurious finish. See page 26.

This cuddly, playful pompom cushion is knitted in a smooth wool mix yarn, while the pompoms are made using three contrasting textures. You could use shop-bought pompoms, but it's much more fun to make your own, and you can create exactly the colours and textures you want. See page 26.

This beautiful variation uses a wonderfully smooth wool/silk mix yarn in a deep green. The sumptuous roses are knitted in three colourways of a hand-dyed variegated yarn in silk. The same yarn is used for the leaves, in a shade of green that complements the background green of the cushion. See page 27.

spring greens

The addition of shop-bought trimmings, such as this lush and tactile ostrich-feather trim, can transform a plain cushion into a glamorous feature of your décor.

Making these cushions is quick and easy. All you need to know is how to cast on, knit and purl to make stockinette stitch, and how to bind off. Two different weights of yarn are used: light-weight (DK) and medium-weight (aran). You could leave the cushions plain or decorate them as I have done.

Shake Your Tail Feather

MEASUREMENTS
16in (40cm) square

GATHER TOGETHER...
Materials
5 x 1¾oz (50g) balls of medium-weight (aran) wool/cashmere knitted tube yarn (83yd/75m per ball) in light olive green
65in (163cm) of dark olive ostrich trim
16in (40cm) cushion pad

Needles
1 pair of size 7 (4.5mm) needles

GAUGE
18 sts and 24 rows to 4in (10cm) square measured over st st (1 row k, 1 row p) using size 7 (4.5mm) needles

Knit your cushion...
Back and Front
(Make 2 the same)
Using size 7 (4.5mm) needles, cast on 72 sts.
Work in st st (1 row k, 1 row p) until work measures 16in (40cm), ending with a p row.
Bind off.

to finish...
Sew in all ends neatly. Press according to instructions on ball bands. Join back and front together around three sides. Insert cushion pad and sew remaining side closed. Sew ostrich-feather trim around the cushion, overlapping ends at one corner.

Sequins and Spangles

MEASUREMENTS
16in (40cm) square

GATHER TOGETHER...
Materials
5 x 1¾oz (50g) balls of medium-weight (aran) viscose/silk yarn (71yd/65m per ball) in light yellow-green
17in (43cm) lengths of ribbons, sequinned or beaded trims
16in (40cm) cushion pad

Needles
1 pair of size 7 (4.5mm) needles

GAUGE
18 sts and 24 rows to 4in (10cm) square measured over st st (1 row k, 1 row p) using size 7 (4.5mm) needles

Knit your cushion...
Back and Front
(Make 2 the same)
Work as given for Shake Your Tail Feather cushion.

to finish...
Sew in all ends neatly. Press according to instructions on ball bands. Sew trims and ribbons onto the front, turning in the raw ends to prevent fraying. Join back and front together around three sides. Insert cushion pad and sew remaining side closed.

Pompom Parade

MEASUREMENTS
16in (40cm) square

GATHER TOGETHER...
Materials
A 5 x 1¾oz (50g) balls of light-weight (DK) wool mix yarn (110yd/100m per ball) in jade
For pompoms: 1 x 1¾oz (50g) ball of each of an astrakhan yarn, a brushed yarn and a slub yarn in shades of green
16in (40cm) cushion pad

Needles
1 pair of size 6 (4mm) needles

GAUGE
22 sts and 28 rows to 4in (10cm) square measured over st st (1 row k, 1 row p) using size 6 (4mm) needles

Knit your cushion...
Back and Front
(Make 2 the same)
Using size 6 (4mm) needles and A, cast on 88 sts.
Work in st st (1 row k, 1 row p) until work measures 16in (40cm), ending with a p row.
Bind off.

to finish...
Sew in all ends neatly. Press according to instructions on ball bands. Using yarn A and the three contrasting yarns, make sufficient pompoms (see page 114) to cover the front of the cushion, using one yarn for a pompom and also mixing two or even three yarns together. Sew onto the front. Join back and front together around three sides. Insert cushion pad and sew remaining side closed.

your yarn, your style!

Buying trims, ribbons and braids is a quick way of finishing; there is a great choice available to suit every taste. Go for bright, funky trims on a hot palette of yarns for a contemporary look, or use darker, richer colours for dramatic interiors (examples shown here). For a more classic effect, choose sugared-almond colours on a palette of soft pastels for a romantic, country look, or a neutral palette with linen, hemp and cotton for a tranquil room.

Floral Fantasy

MEASUREMENTS
16in (40cm) square

GATHER TOGETHER...
Materials

A 4 x 1¾oz (50g) balls of light-weight (DK) silk/ wool yarn (131yd/120m per ball) in dark green
B For roses: 3 x 11yd (10m) skeins of hand-dyed silk thread (equivalent to light-weight/DK yarn) in each of three colourways of pinks/fuchsias/mauves
C For leaves: 2 x 11yd (10m) skeins of hand-dyed silk thread (equivalent to light-weight/DK yarn) in colourway of greens
16in (40cm) cushion pad

Needles
1 pair of size 6 (4mm) needles
1 pair of size 7 (4.5mm) needles

GAUGE
22 sts and 28 rows to 4in (10cm) measured over st st (1 row k, 1 row p) using size 6 (4mm) needles

Knit your cushion...
Back and Front
(Make 2 the same)
Work as given for Pompom Parade cushion.

to finish...
Sew in all ends. Press according to instructions on ball bands. Make 9 roses and 11 leaves (see page 115 for pattern). Sew roses in a square three roses wide by three roses high in the centre of the front. Sew the leaves around the roses. Join back and front together around three sides. Insert cushion pad and sew remaining side closed.

IN THE MIX
A Light-weight (DK) mercerized cotton in hot pink
B Light-weight (DK) wool/silk mix in spicy orange
C Medium-weight (aran) wool tweed in lipstick pink
D Medium-weight (aran) wool in hot orange

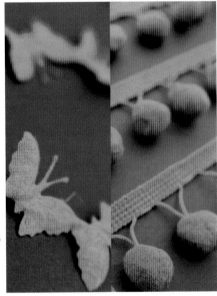

IN THE MIX
A Light-weight (DK) silk/wool mix in dark mauve
B Light-weight (DK) wool tweed in wine red
C Medium-weight (aran) pure wool in dark purple
D Medium-weight (aran) cashmere/wool mix in rich red

DESIGN SECRETS UNRAVELLED…

Make a collection of cushions around
a simple colour palette and decorate
them in different ways – you can work
some dynamic changes through the
addition of the various trimmings.
Alternatively, you could knit just one
cushion to add a splash of colour
to an interior.

*Using one basic colourway
to make a range of cushions
is a lovely way of introducing
subtle, harmonious colour
into a room setting. Adding
different embellishments to
each cushion is a great way to
introduce interest and variety
while maintaining the integrity
of the overall co-ordinated look.*

YARN FOCUS

I chose green as the predominant
colour for these cushions; these greens
are fresh and leafy, but also warm
and down-to-earth colours, so they're
quite versatile. You could make all four
cushions and display them together;
using one basic colour palette will
create visual harmony despite the
different yarns used for each cushion.

green silk/wool

variegated leaf

jade green wool

green slub yarn

dark astrakhan

jade green wool

green slub yarn

variegated leaf

dark astrakhan

terrific trimmings

One of the great things about knitting is that you can take a fairly plain knitted fabric in one main colour and embellish it with shop-bought trimmings such as sequins and beads. In this chapter I've focused on yarns that produce a rich and tactile texture; a wool and silk blend was used for the throw shown here, and a vibrant ribbon yarn for the cushion on pages 34–35. I decided to enhance these yarns by adding glamorous large sequins to the sophisticated throw, and fun, funky plastic beads for the kitschy cushion. The marriage of yarn and trimming is a great source of creativity.

Here the lush sheen of the deep purple fabric is perfectly complemented by the reflective gold and deep red paillettes. The addition of a fringe in the main yarn and two flashing metallic yarns is the perfect complementary touch.

DESIGN SECRETS UNRAVELLED...

Because the throw is chair-sized, and therefore smaller than a bed-sized throw, you could indulge in some luxurious yarn. Choose silk mixes to give the fabric a lustrous sheen or use cashmere or velvet chenille for touchable elegance. The large sequins are available in other metallic colours such as silver, bronze and copper; combine them with dramatic dark wine-red, emerald green or midnight blue. For a lighter touch for a throw to drape over a bedroom chair, choose transparent sequins with a hint of lilac or rose and set them against pale mint-green silk.

YARN FOCUS

I wanted a luxurious evening throw – something to drape over a chair that would reflect the glow of candles. This throw is worked in a silk and wool yarn in a deep, rich purple. The large gold sequins are knitted into the fabric around the edges of the throw to form a shimmering border. A mixture of gold and wine-red sequins create glinting flashes of colour amid the long fringe.

silk

dark purple silk

metallic sequins

allic

purple metallic

gold metallic

sequinned shimmer

MEASUREMENTS
24in (61cm) wide and 36in (91.5cm) long
(excluding fringe)

GATHER TOGETHER...
Materials
A 10 x 1¾oz (50g) balls of medium-weight (aran)
wool/silk yarn (98yd/90m per ball) in dark purple
1 x ⁷⁄₈oz (25g) ball of fine-weight (4ply) metallic
yarn (104yd/95m per ball) in gold **B** and purple **C**

Approx 500 gold and 200 wine 1in (24mm)
flat sequins or paillettes with large hole at top

Needles and notions
1 pair of size 9 (5.5mm) needles
1 size B1 (2.50mm) crochet hook

GAUGE
18 sts and 26 rows to 4in (10cm) measured over
st st (1 row k, 1 row p) using size 9 (5.5mm)
needles and yarn A

*Knit Note: The hole in the sequins (paillettes)
should be big enough for two strands of yarn
to go through. Make a bigger hole if necessary
using a hole punch.*

SPECIAL ABBREVIATIONS
PB Place sequin by inserting crochet hook through
hole in sequin, hook next st off the left-hand
needle and through the sequin. Place the st onto
the right-hand needle without working it.

*The fringe is made from three yarns: the yarn
used for the main body of the throw, a metallic
purple yarn, and a metallic gold yarn.*

This throw is a simple rectangle knitted in stockinette stitch in a beautifully lush medium-weight (aran) wool and silk mix yarn. The design impact comes from the large gold sequins (paillettes) that are knitted in to create a border as you work. The fringe is added later; it is made with the main yarn, together with two metallic yarns, and decorated with both gold and wine-red sequins.

Knit your throw...
PB: Use large gold sequins (paillettes) throughout.
Using size 9 (5.5mm) needles and A, cast on
109 sts.

Lower border
Work 6 rows in st st, starting with a k row.
Bead Row 1 K3, PB, (k5, PB) 17 times, k3.
Work 5 rows in st st.
**Bead Row 2 K6, PB, (k5, PB) 16 times, k6.
Work 5 rows in st st.
Bead Row 3 K3, PB, (k5, PB) 17 times, k3.
Work 5 rows in st st.**
Rep from ** to ** once more.
Work 5 rows in st st.

Side borders and centre panel
Bead Row 6 K6, PB, (k5, PB) twice, k71, PB, (k5, PB) twice, k6.
Work 5 rows in st st.
***Bead Row 7 K3, PB, (k5, PB) 3 times, k65, PB, (k3, PB) 3 times, k3.
Work 5 rows in st st.
Bead Row 8 K6, PB, (k5, PB) twice, k71, PB, (k5, PB) twice, k6.
Work 5 rows in st st.***
Rep from *** to *** until throw measures approx
31in (79cm) from beg.

Top border
Work Bead Row 1 once more.
Work 5 rows in st st.
Rep from ** to ** twice.
Bind off.

to finish...
Sew in all ends neatly.

Fringe
Using A, wrap the yarn loosely around a piece of cardboard 12in (30cm) wide several times. Cut the wrapped strands at the bottom and remove the cardboard. Repeat for yarns B and C. Take two lengths of A and one length of B and fold in half. Using a crochet hook, pull the strands through the edge of the throw at one corner from front to back by catching the fold with the hook. Pass the ends through the folded loop and pull to tighten the knot. Make another tassel 1in (2.5cm) away from the first, using two lengths of A and one length of C. Continue in this way around the throw, alternating B and C with two strands of A, making each tassel 1in (2.5cm) apart.

Starting at one corner, take three strands from the first tassel and three strands from the next tassel and tie together with an overhand knot approx 1in (2.5cm) from the edge of the throw. Continue around the throw. Decorate the fringe by tying one gold and one wine sequin onto each tassel, use the crochet hook to pull the yarn through the holes.

Each sequin (paillette) is hooked into place with a crochet hook. This is quite a slow process, but creates a stunning effect.

your yarn, your style!

Finding the perfect combination of yarn and sequin trim should give your imagination plenty to feed on. Go for a lighter-toned variation of pale blue or pink with iridescent sequins, or set off brown and sage yarns with warm copper or gold sequins.

IN THE MIX
A Medium-weight (aran) cotton chenille in pale sage green
B Light-weight (DK) metallic ladder tape in shades of copper, bronze and gold. Dark bronze sequins

IN THE MIX
A Medium-weight (aran) cotton/silk tweed in shades of brown
B Light-weight (DK) metallic ladder tape in shades of copper, bronze and gold. Gold sequins

bead me up!

MEASUREMENTS
14in (35.5cm) square

GATHER TOGETHER...
Materials
3 x 1¾oz (50g) balls of bulky-weight ribbon yarn
(87yd/80m per ball) in bright lime green
Pony beads in heart, star and barrel shapes –
8 of each shape in purple, yellow and pink
14in (35.5cm) cushion pad

Needles and notions
1 pair of size 10 (6mm) needles
1 size B1 (2.50mm) crochet hook

GAUGE
16 sts and 18 rows to 4in (10cm)
measured over st st (1 row k, 1 row p)
using size 10 (6mm) needles

SPECIAL ABBREVIATIONS
PB Place bead by inserting crochet hook through
bead from top to bottom, hook next st off the left-
hand needle and through the bead. Place the st
onto the right-hand needle without working it.

lime green ribbon

pretty pony beads

YARN FOCUS
For this project I chose the beads first; these
bright plastic beads are made for children
but also make for a great kitschy textile.
I wanted a yarn in a bright colour with a hard
contemporary feel and found this bold glossy
ribbon in an amazing zingy lime. The beads
and the yarn clash wonderfully, and this
cushion would provide a stab of colour in
a sharp-edged urban apartment.

Like the Sequinned Shimmer throw, this cushion is simply knitted in stockinette stitch. It is made in two square pieces that are sewn shut once the cushion pad has been inserted. This fun, bold cushion is decorated with rows of brightly coloured pony beads, which are knitted into the fabric as you work.

Knit your cushion...
Front
Using size 10 (6mm) needles, cast on 57 sts.
Work 4in (10cm) in st st (1 row k, 1 row p).
**Bead Row 1 (Purple hearts) K14, PB, (k3, PB)
7 times, k to end.
Work 3 rows in st st.
Bead Row 2 (Pink stars) K16, PB, (k3, PB) 6 times,
k to end.
Work 3 rows in st st.**
Rep from ** to ** 3 times more then rep Bead Row
1 once more, using beads in the following order:
yellow barrels, purple stars, pink barrels, yellow
hearts, purple barrels, pink hearts, yellow stars.
Work in st st until front measures 14in (35.5cm),
ending with a p row.
Bind off.

DESIGN SECRETS UNRAVELLED...
You could use pink heart-shaped beads on
a pale pink fabric for a really feminine cushion,
or bright yellow stars on silver for a space-age
textile. These beads would also look great on
a bold, bright cotton for a child's room. They are
available in other shapes too; use animal shapes,
glow-in-the-dark, or glitter beads.

Back
Using size 10 (6mm) needles, cast on 57 sts and
work 14in (35.5cm) in st st, ending with a p row.
Bind off.

to finish...
Sew in all ends neatly. Press according to
instructions on ball band. Sew front to back around
three edges. Insert cushion pad and sew remaining
edge closed.

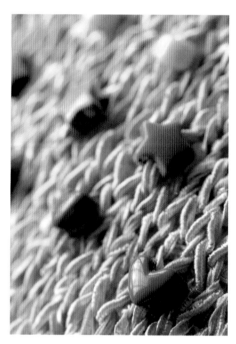

The plastic beads in chunky, kitschy moulded shapes make a fabulously vivid contrast when set against the lime-green knitted fabric.

celtic knot garden

This large and hard-wearing cushion can be used as a floor cushion or outdoors. The design contains many allusions to the natural world. The variegated wool yarn is full of rustic colours that reminded me of woodland, lichen and moss. The cable pattern that looks like intertwined branches on the top of the cushion is reminiscent of Celtic knot gardens, a very traditional style of garden design that is centuries old. This is a beautiful, timeless design that would work equally well on an old stone bench or to add a warm and earthy accent to an uncluttered, neutral interior.

Cable stitches tend to work best in a smooth yarn such as wool so the raised pattern can be clearly seen against the knitted background. Here the knitting has also been felted to transform the texture of the fabric and make the cable pattern stand out even more.

DESIGN SECRETS UNRAVELLED...

Felting alters the cable pattern completely, making it into almost free-standing intertwining tubes.
If you don't want to felt it, choose wool with a high twist or cotton that will produce a tough fabric. Have a look at natural undyed wool, especially that from breeds of mountain or hill sheep; maybe you have a local producer. Natural wool comes in a great range of shades from cream through grey to very dark brown. As well as merged stone or earthy colours, this cushion would look fantastic as a single graphic block of colour; how about dark chocolate for a loft-style city apartment, or bright orange for a retro 1960s look? If you can't find the perfect colour in a bulky-weight yarn, you could use two or three strands of a thinner yarn.

YARN FOCUS

I chose this yarn because it contained just the shades I wanted: natural, earthy colours including stone, green, brown and rust. Because it is a loosely spun single yarn, I knew it would not be hard-wearing enough for a floor or outdoor cushion. Yarns like this are great for bulky-weight soft sweaters, but not for pieces that will get a lot of wear and tear. The solution was to felt the knitted fabric. This changed it completely; it lost its loftiness and became a strong, textured fabric in merged shades resembling lichen-covered stone. The cable looks like a deeply chiselled sculpture – fantastic for an outdoor cushion.

shades of stone

woodland greens

earthy hues

woodland greens

earthy hues

celtic knot garden

MEASUREMENTS
Before felting: Top measures approx
23in (58.5cm) long and 24in (61cm) wide
Finished size: 22in (56cm) square and
4in (10cm) deep

GATHER TOGETHER...
Materials
14 x 1¾oz (50g) balls of bulky-weight
wool yarn (55yd/50m per ball) in shades
of stone, green and brown
4in (10cm)-deep seating foam block cut to size
after felting (or knitting is completed)
Fabric to cover foam block
Strong sewing thread in matching colour

Needles
1 pair of size 13 (9mm) needles
Cable needle

GAUGE
10 sts and 14 rows to 4in (10cm) measured
over st st (1 row k, 1 row p) using
size 13 (9mm) needles

SPECIAL ABBREVIATIONS
C8B Slip 4 sts on to cable needle at back,
k4, k4 from cable needle

C8F Slip 4 sts on to cable needle at front,
k4, k4 from cable needle

Cr6L Slip 4 sts on to cable needle at front,
p2, k4 from cable needle

Cr6R Slip 2 sts on to cable needle at back,
k4, p2 from cable needle

Cr5L Slip 4 sts on to cable needle at front,
p1, k4 from cable needle

Cr5R Slip 1 st on to cable needle at back,
k4, p1 from cable needle

*Knit Note: The pattern instructions refer
to seed stitch. This is a US term; non-US
knitters know this stitch as moss stitch*

This cushion is made in three pieces: the top and the side piece are knitted, and the base is made out of fabric. The side piece and the edges of the top panel are worked in seed stitch (non-US: moss stitch), which creates a bumpy, textured pattern, while the cable design is set against a background of reverse stockinette stitch. The knitted pieces are felted to make the woollen fabric more dense and robust. The base of the cushion is covered with hard-wearing fabric.

Knit your cushion...
Top
Using size 13 (9mm) needles, cast on 53 sts.
Row 1 K1, *p1, k1; rep from * to end.
Rep this row 6 times more.
Inc Row (WS) K1, (p1, k1) 3 times, M1, p1, (M1, k1, p1) 19 times, M1, k1, (p1, k1) 3 times. 74 sts.

Begin cable panel.
Row 1 (K1, p1) 3 times, k5, p6, k4, p12, k8, p12, k4, p6, k5, (p1, k1) 3 times.
Row 2 K1, (p1, k1) 3 times, p4, k6, p4, k12, p8, k12, p4, k6, p4, k1, (p1, k1) 3 times.
Row 3 As row 1.
Row 4 As row 2.
Row 5 (K1, p1) 3 times, k5, p6, k4, p12, C8B, p12, k4, p6, k5, (p1, k1) 3 times.
Row 6 As row 2.
Row 7 (K1, p1) 3 times, k5, p6, (Cr6L, p8, Cr6R) twice, p6, k5, (p1, k1) 3 times.
Row 8 K1, (p1, k1) 3 times, (p4, k8) twice, p4, k4, (p4, k8) twice, p4, k1, (p1, k1) 3 times.
Row 9 (K1, p1) 3 times, k5, p8, (Cr6L, p4, Cr6R, p4) twice, p4, k5, (p1, k1) 3 times.
Row 10 K1, (p1, k1) 3 times, p4, k10, p4, k4, p4, k8, p4, k4, p4, k10, p4, k1, (p1, k1) 3 times.
Row 11 (K1, p1) 3 times, k5, p10, (Cr6L, Cr6R, p8) twice, p2, k5, (p1, k1) 3 times.
Row 12 K1, (p1, k1) 3 times, p4, (k12, p8) twice, k12, p4, k1, (p1, k1) 3 times.
Row 13 K1, (p1, k1) 3 times, Cr5L, p11, C8F, p12, C8F, p11, Cr5R, k1, (p1, k1) 3 times.
Row 14 (K1, p1) 3 times, k2, p4, k11, p8, k12, p8, k11, p4, k2, (p1, k1) 3 times.
Row 15 (K1, p1) 4 times, Cr5L, p8, (Cr6R, Cr6L, p8)

twice, Cr5R, (p1, k1) 4 times.
Row 16 (K1, p1) 3 times, k3, p4, k8, p4, k4, p4, k8, p4, k4, p4, k8, p4, k3, (p1, k1) 3 times.
Row 17 K1, (p1, k1) 3 times, p2, (Cr6L, p4, Cr6R, p4) twice, Cr6L, p4, Cr6R, p2, k1, (p1, k1) 3 times.
Row 18 (K1, p1) 3 times, k5, (p4, k4, p4, k8) twice,

Seed stitch creates a wonderfully organic-looking fabric with lots of deep texture.

p4, k4, p4, k5, (p1, k1) 3 times.

Row 19 K1, (p1, k1) 3 times, p4, (Cr6L, Cr6R, p8) twice, Cr6L, Cr6R, p4, k1, (p1, k1) 3 times.

Row 20 (K1, p1) 3 times, k7, (p8, k12) twice, p8, k7, (p1, k1) 3 times.

Row 21 K1, (p1, k1) 3 times, p6, (C8B, p12) twice, C8B, p6, k1, (p1, k1) 3 times.

Row 22 As row 20.

Row 23 K1, (p1, k1) 3 times, p4, (Cr6R, Cr6L, p8) twice, Cr6R, Cr6L, p4, k1, (p1, k1) 3 times.

Row 24 As row 18.

Row 25 K1, (p1, k1) 3 times, p2, (Cr6R, p4, Cr6L, p4) twice, Cr6R, p4, Cr6L, p2, k1, (p1, k1) 3 times.

Row 26 As row 16.

Row 27 (K1, p1) 4 times, Cr5R, (p8, Cr6L, Cr6R) twice, p8, Cr5L, (p1, k1) 4 times.

Row 28 As row 14.

Row 29 K1, (p1, k1) 3 times, Cr5R, p11, C8F, p12, C8F, p11, Cr5L, k1, (p1, k1) 3 times.

Row 30 As row 12.

Row 31 (K1, p1) 3 times, k5, p10, Cr6R, Cr6L, p8, Cr6R, Cr6L, p10, k5, (p1, k1) 3 times.

Row 32 As row 10.

Row 33 (K1, p1) 3 times, k5, p8, (Cr6R, p4, Cr6L, p4) twice, p4, k5, (p1, k1) 3 times.

Row 34 As row 8.

Row 35 (K1, p1) 3 times, k5, p6, (Cr6R, p8, Cr6L) twice, p6, k5, (p1, k1) 3 times.

Row 36 As row 6.

Rep from row 5 to row 36 once more.

Row 69 As row 5.

Row 70 As row 2.

Row 71 As row 1.

Rep last 2 rows again.

Dec Row K1, (p1, k1) 3 times, p2tog, k2tog, (p1, k2tog) 18 times, p2tog, k1, (p1, k1) 3 times. 53 sts.

Next Row K1, *p1, k1; rep from * to end.

Rep this row 6 times more.

Bind off.

Side piece

Using size 13 (9mm) needles, cast on 13 sts.

Row 1 K1, *p1, k1; rep from * to end.

Rep this row, forming seed stitch, until sides measure 108in (274cm) long.

Bind off.

To finish...

Sew in all ends neatly. Following the instructions for fulling on page 120, felt the top and side pieces until the top measures 22in (56cm) square or the fabric has felted sufficiently. Dry the pieces, pulling the top into a square and straightening the edges of the side piece.

Foam insert

Measure the width and length of the top; have a 4in (10cm)-deep piece of foam cut to these measurements. Cover the foam with a fabric slip cover, using a hard-wearing canvas or fake suede fabric for the base (see pages 118–119 for covering cushions).

The base of the cushion is made from tough fabric to withstand wear and tear.

Making up the cushion

On the side piece, measure 22in (56cm) (or length of top) from one end and place a marker. Measure another 22in (56cm) (or width of top) and place another marker. Rep this twice more for the other two sides (measure length and then width of top). If you have extra fabric at the end, do not cut it off until the cushion has been made up. Beginning at bottom right corner, pin the side piece to the top, matching the marker with top right corner. Sew into place. Match the second marker with the top left corner and sew second side in place. Repeat for other two sides. Sew the two ends of the side piece together and cut off any excess fabric. Pull onto foam insert, matching corners and seams. Pin the knitted fabric onto the foam, pulling so the sides are completely covered. Using strong sewing thread, sew the knitted fabric to the base fabric.

sizzling stripes

Vibrant, rich colours like red and purple make a dramatic statement in any interior. Here I've made the most of these high-impact colours by working them in stripes of many shades; the bolster is worked in a pattern of wide stripes in dark reds separated by brighter narrow stripes, and the circular cushion is worked in a smaller range of purples separated by glittering metallic bands. These pieces are knitted in the round using double-pointed needles and a circular needle. If you've never knitted in the round before, take the plunge; it will increase your repertoire and give you more chances to create fantastic finishing touches.

Using a number of yarns in different shades of rich and vivid reds creates a fantastically fiery fabric.

DESIGN SECRETS UNRAVELLED…

For a fresher, lighter look, you could collect together shades of spring greens or aqua blues. A palette of soft browns and chocolates would look very sophisticated, while a collection of bright, hot colours would be ideal for a contemporary interior. You could use different textures for the wide stripes and contrast them with smoother yarns for the narrow stripes. The pattern can easily be adapted for different size cushion pads; the round cushion (page 43) shows you how to carry on increasing for a wider diameter, and the tube between can be worked to any length.

YARN FOCUS

I wanted this bolster to be luxurious, rich and glamorous, so I chose a palette of deep reds. It is amazing how many shades of red are available, so you should have no problem collecting together seven dark reds and contrasting them with four shades of bright red. I added a metallic red to the mix as well for an extra touch of opulence. For the wide stripes, I used seven dark, rich reds in light-weight (DK) and medium-weight (aran) yarns: two wool yarns in light and dark raspberry, three shades of dark red wool, a textured yarn in wine, and a dark burgundy wool. The narrow stripes are worked in four yarns: two wool yarns in bright scarlet and fiery red, a pale red mercerized cotton, and a glittery metallic red yarn.

dark wine red

dark raspberry

burgundy   light raspberry

scarlet   rich red

raspberry   textured wine

fiery red

metallic red

brilliant bolster

MEASUREMENTS

7in (18cm) diameter and 18½in (47cm) long

GATHER TOGETHER...
Materials

A 1 x 1¾oz (50g) ball of light-weight (DK)
or medium-weight (aran) yarn in each of seven
shades of dark red and burgundy
B 1 x 1¾oz (50g) ball of light-weight (DK)
or medium-weight (aran) yarn in each of three
shades of scarlet and light red
1 x ⅞oz (25g) ball of fine-weight (4ply)
metallic yarn in red
Bolster cushion pad 7in (18cm) diameter
and 18½in (47cm) long

Needles

1 set of size 6 (4mm) double-pointed needles
1 size 6 (4mm) 16in (40cm)-long circular needle

GAUGE

22 sts and 28 rows to 4in (10cm) measured
over st st (1 row k, 1 row p) using size 6 (4mm)
needles and A

Knit Note:

*Yarns A: use these in any order, using one yarn
for each wide stripe.*

*Yarns B: Also use these randomly, although I did
use the metallic yarn for every third stripe and
mixed the others for the two stripes between.*

*Use two strands of metallic yarn together
throughout. Make sure that you work through
both strands for each stitch.*

Bolster cushions always seem more opulent to me than the more usual square forms. This cushion has two circular motifs for the ends, linked by a tube of circular knitting between. Worked in a simple stripe pattern, this is a great project to begin using double-pointed and circular needles if you have never tried this before. You use only knit stitch, and the increases are simply worked by knitting into the front and back of a stitch.

Knit your bolster...
Bolster ends
(Make 2)

Using size 6 (4mm) double-pointed needles and yarn A, cast on 8 sts and arrange them on four needles.

Round 1 Using A, k8. Place a marker to show end of rnd, slip this marker on every rnd.
Round 2 Using A, (kf&b) into each st. 16 sts.
Rounds 3, 4 and 5 Using A, k to end.
Round 6 Using A, (kf&b) into each st. 32 sts.
Rounds 7, 8 and 9 Using A, k to end.
Round 10 Using A, *k1, kf&b; rep from * to end. 48 sts.
Rounds 11 and 12 Using B, k to end.
Round 13 Using A, k to end.
Round 14 Using A, *k2, kf&b; rep from * to end. 64 sts.
Rounds 15, 16 and 17 Using A, k to end.
Round 18 Using A, *k3, kf&b; rep from * to end. 80 sts.
Rounds 19, 20 and 21 Using A, k to end.
Round 22 Using A, *k4, kf&b; rep from * to end. 96 sts.
Rounds 23 and 24 Using B, k to end.
Round 25 Using A, k to end.
Round 26 Using A, *k5, kf&b; rep from * to end. 112 sts.
Rounds 27 and 28 Using A, k to end.
Bind off loosely.

Bolster tube

With RS of work facing, using size 6 (4mm) circular needle and A, pick up and knit 112 sts around the edge of one bolster end. Place a marker to show end of round.
Using A, knit 9 rounds.
**Using B, knit 2 rounds.
Using A, knit 10 rounds.
Rep from ** until side measures approx 18½in (47cm) long, ending with 10 rows of A.
Bind off loosely.

to finish...

Sew in all ends neatly. Press according to instructions on ball bands. Insert bolster cushion pad. Sew circular end to bound-off edge of side.

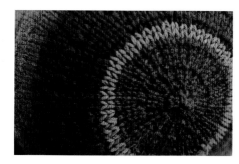

*The circular shape of the bolster ends is made
by increasing stitches at marked points on every
fourth row.*

MEASUREMENTS

14in (36cm) diameter

GATHER TOGETHER...
Materials

A 2 x 1¾oz (50g) balls of light-weight (DK) yarn (131yd/120m per ball) in light purple

B 1 x 1¾oz (50g) ball of light-weight (DK) yarn (175yd/160m per ball) in dark purple

C 2 x ⅞oz (25g) balls of light-weight (DK) metallic yarn (110yd/100m per ball) in purple
Cushion pad 14in (36cm) in diameter

Needles

1 set of size 6 (4mm) double-pointed needles
1 size 6 (4mm) 16in (40cm)-long circular needle

GAUGE

22 sts and 28 rows to 4in (10cm) measured over st st (1 row k, 1 row p) using size 6 (4mm) needles and A

Knit Note: Yarn C uses two strands together throughout. Make sure that you work through both strands for each stitch.

Knit Note: Transfer the work onto the circular needle when you have sufficient stitches.

purple metallic

pale purple wool

rich cotton mix

YARN FOCUS

Purple is a fantastic colour for dramatic interiors. I've used only two shades of purple for this round cushion, alternating them to make a pattern of concentric circles separated by a wonderful metallic purple yarn.

This round cushion uses a larger version of the bolster cushion ends to make two circular motifs that are then sewn together.

DESIGN SECRETS UNRAVELLED...

For another idea, use five different shades to work each of the wide stripes. Or you could work the cushion in one main colour and use a textured or beaded yarn for the narrow stripes.

Knit your cushion...
Front and Back

(Make 2)

Work rounds 1 to 28 as given for Bolster Ends, working rounds 11 and 12, 23 and 24 in C, and rounds 13 to 22 in B.

Round 29 Using A, k to end.

Round 30 Using A, *k6, kf&b; rep from * to end. 128 sts.

Rounds 31, 32 and 33 Using A, k to end.

Round 34 Using A, *k7, kf&b; rep from * to end. 144 sts.

Rounds 35 and 36 Using C, k to end.

Round 37 Using B, k to end.

Round 38 Using B, *k8, kf&b; rep from * to end. 160 sts.

Rounds 39, 40 and 41 Using A, k to end.

Round 42 Using B, *k9, kf&b; rep from * to end. 176 sts.

Rounds 43, 44 and 45 Using A, k to end.

Round 46 Using B, *k10, kf&b; rep from * to end. 192 sts.

Rounds 47 and 48 Using C, k to end.

Round 49 Using A, k to end.

Round 50 Using A, *k11, kf&b; rep from * to end. 208 sts.

Rounds 51, 52 and 53 Using A, k to end.

Round 54 Using A, *k12, kf&b; rep from * to end. 224 sts.

Rounds 55, 56 and 57 Using A, k to end.
Bind off loosely.

to finish...

Sew in all ends neatly. Press according to instructions on ball bands. Sew back to front leaving a large gap. Insert cushion pad. Sew gap closed.

Here, just two shades of purple are used, with a narrow band of glinting metallic yarn worked in between each stripe.

mixing it up

The table runner shown here and the vibrantly colourful cushion shown on pages 48–49 are two designs that are a showcase for texture. The aim of these projects is to expand your ideas about what media and materials you can use to knit with. Both the runner and the cushion are knitted using a mixture of traditional yarns, such as mercerized cotton and bouclé yarn, incorporated with more innovative media such as braids, lace, string, sequins and fabric. I wanted to show that almost anything can be used to create a unique knitted fabric – with some truly stunning results.

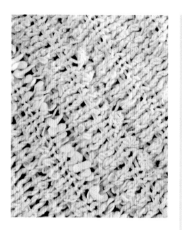

A close-up of the knitted fabric shows what rich and fascinating textures can be achieved by using such a wide variety of materials.

YARN FOCUS

I wanted to use a limited palette of cream and undyed ecru yarns in dry matte yarns – I also knew this would give me a large range of other, more unusual, materials to work with. Almost all yarn ranges include a shade of cream or a natural hue, so it was easy to source a mix of seven textures, including a velour tape, a thin braid, natural and mercerized cottons, bouclé yarn, a textured cotton/silk mix and some undyed parcel string. The other media that I used were a braid of daisies and a braid of circles, two widths of ricrac braid, lace, and calico fabric cut into strips.

DESIGN SECRETS UNRAVELLED...

The more traditional knitting yarns are used for working the greater part of the runner, while the other media are worked as single-row stripes. Have a look in haberdashery and charity shops for braids, ribbons and trims that are narrow enough and malleable enough to knit with. Check out hardware shops for string in different fibres and colours, and fabric shops for fabrics that can be cut into strips narrow enough to knit with. You can use one basic shade as I have done – collect your media together first to make sure you can obtain enough materials in your chosen colour. Alternatively, choose a range of colours to fit in with your interior; pastels, neutrals or brights.

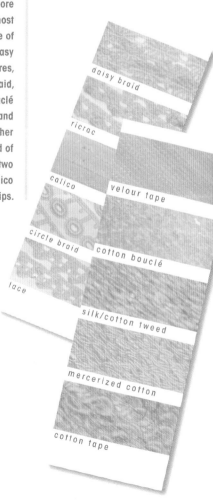

daisy braid

ricrac

calico

velour tape

circle braid

cotton bouclé

lace

silk/cotton tweed

mercerized cotton

cotton tape

mixed messages

MEASUREMENTS
9½in wide and 55in long (24 by 140cm)

GATHER TOGETHER…
Materials
Yarns
A 1 x 1¾oz (50g) ball of medium-weight (aran) silk mix yarn (118yd/108m per ball) in cream
B 1 x 1¾oz (50g) ball of medium-weight (aran) cotton tape (55yd/50m per ball) in cream
C 1 x 1¾oz (50g) ball of light-weight (DK) undyed cotton yarn (102yd/93m per ball)
D 1 x 1¾oz (50g) ball of light-weight (DK) velour tape (64yd/58m per ball) in cream
E 1 x 1¾oz (50g) ball of light-weight (DK) cotton bouclé (137yd/125m per ball) in cream
F 1 x 3½oz (100g) ball of light-weight (DK) cotton yarn (230yd/210m per ball) in cream
G 1 x ball of undyed cotton parcel string

Braids
6½yd (6m) of each of five braids including lace, daisy braid, ricrac braid
½yd (50cm) length of calico fabric
(you will need to cut this into a strip narrow enough to knit with before you start)

Unvarnished oval wood beads

Needles
1 size 10½ (6.5mm) 40in (100cm)-long circular needle

GAUGE
12 sts and 22 rows (average) to 4in (10cm) square measured over st st (1 row k, 1 row p) using size 10½ (6.5mm) needles and working 1 row in each of yarns A, B, C, D, E, F and G.

Knit Note: *The circular needle is used to accommodate the large number of sts, not for circular knitting. Turn work after every row.*

This table runner is worked in stockinette stitch with garter-stitch borders. Most of the project is worked in one of the seven traditional knitting yarns; these are interspersed with single rows worked in the more unusual media (identified as 'Braid Row' in the pattern instructions). The runner is self-fringing; the fringe is made as you work by leaving long tails of yarn at each end of every row. Extra interest is added by threading beads randomly onto sections of the fringe.

Prepare your project…
Some of the media need to be prepared before you can knit with them. For example, you will need to cut the calico fabric into a continuous strip 1in (2.5cm) wide. Do this by cutting across the width, stopping 1in (2.5cm) from the edge. Begin cutting from this edge 1in (2.5cm) above the last cut line and cut across the width in the other direction to the other edge, stopping 1in (2.5cm) from the edge. Either leave the strips as they are with raw edges that will fray, or neaten them as I did for this project. Using a sewing machine set on zigzag, fold the strip in half and sew through both thicknesses along the raw edges to neaten.

To make a textured yarn to use for a braid row, I used the mercerized cotton (yarn F) to make a long crocheted chain. Use an E4 (3.50mm) crochet hook and work in chain stitch. You could use this method to thicken a thin yarn so it matches the correct gauge.

Knit your table runner…
Using size 10½ (6.5mm) circular needle and yarn A, cast on 160 sts leaving a long tail of at least 8in (20cm) at both ends.
Next Row Leaving a tail of approx 8in (20cm), join in yarn B by knotting it together with the long tail from previous row, knit to end, cut yarn leaving a long tail.
Next Row Leaving a tail of similar length, join in yarn C by knotting it together with the long tail from previous row, knit to end, cut yarn leaving a long tail.
Cont as set, knitting 1 row in each of yarns D, E, F, G and A.
Braid Row Leaving a tail of similar length, join in any braid by knotting it together with the long tail from previous row, knit to end, cut braid leaving a long tail.
**The next 7 rows are worked in the yarns, use them in any order as follows:
Next Row Leaving a tail of similar length, join in the next yarn by knotting it together with the long tail from previous row, k6, p to last 6 sts, k6, cut yarn leaving a long tail.
Next Row Leaving a tail of similar length, join in the next yarn by knotting it together with the long tail from previous row, knit to end, cut yarn leaving a long tail.
Rep these 2 rows twice more.

Next Row Leaving a tail of similar length, join in the next yarn by knotting it together with the long tail from previous row, k6, p to last 6 sts, k6, cut yarn leaving a long tail.
Braid Row Leaving a tail of similar length, join in another braid by knotting it together with the long tail from previous row, knit to end, cut braid leaving a long tail.**
Rep from ** to ** 4 times more.
Knit 7 rows, using only the seven yarns in any order.
Using A, bind off loosely.

to finish...
Press according to instructions on ball bands. Thread the beads at random onto the fringe, preventing them from slipping off by tying a small knot beneath each one. Trim the fringe if desired.

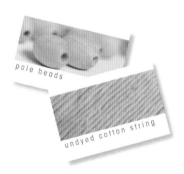

pale beads

undyed cotton string

YARN FOCUS
The different textures together create a really dry, crisp fabric. For a warmer-looking table runner suitable for winter, use wool yarns and fluffy yarns such as angora and mohair. Knit in strips of tweed fabric and wool flannel together with woven woollen braids, or add beaded and sequinned braids for a festive Christmas fabric.

The fringe shows off the wonderful variety of different materials and textures that feature in the runner.

colour carnival

MEASUREMENTS

Rectangular piece is 36in (90 cm) by 16in 40cm); sewn-up cushion is 16in (40cm) square

GATHER TOGETHER...
Materials
Yarns

A 1 x 1¾oz (50g) ball of light-weight (DK) cotton/silk mix yarn (109yd/100m per ball) in hot pink

B 1 x 1¾oz (50g) ball of medium-weight (aran) multi-stranded tape and slub yarn (79yd/72m per ball) in turquoise/green

C 1 x ⅞oz (25g) ball of light-weight (DK) sequinned yarn (73yd/67m per ball) in turquoise

D 1 x 1¾oz (50g) ball of medium-weight (aran) eyelash yarn (90yd/85m per ball) in turquoise

E 1 x 1¾oz (50g) ball of medium-weight (aran) ribbon (87yd/79m per ball) in lime green

F 1 x 3½oz (100g) ball of medium-weight (aran) silk yarn (163yd/149m per ball) in shades of pink

G 40in (1m) of pink nylon net cut into ½in (1.5cm) wide strips (see Prepare your project, page 46)

Braids

5½yd (5m) of each of ten braids including ribbons, cords, ricrac braids, strips of sequins

Medium-weight eyelash yarn in bright pink – use an H8 (5.00mm) crochet hook to work a 5½yd (5m) length in chain stitch

16in (40cm) cushion pad

Needles

1 size 10½ (6.5mm) 40in (100cm)-long circular needle

GAUGE

14 sts and 21 rows (average) to 4in (10cm) square measured over st st (1 row k, 1 row p) using size 10½ (6.5mm) circular needle and working 1 row in each of yarns A, B, C, D, E, F and G.

Knit Note: *Yarns A and C use two strands together. Work through all strands for each stitch.*

Like the Mixed Messages runner, this cushion is knitted in stockinette stitch with garter stitch borders and is self-fringing. The cushion is envelope style; it is worked in one piece and the flap folds over to hide the cushion pad inside.

Knit your cushion...

Using size 10½ (6.5mm) circular needle and A, cast on 114 sts leaving a long tail of at least 8in (20cm).

Next Row Leaving a tail of approx 8in (20cm), join in yarn B by knotting it together with the long tail from previous row, knit to end, cut yarn leaving a long tail.

Next Row Leaving a tail of similar length, join in yarn C by knotting it together with the long tail from previous row, knit to end, cut yarn leaving a long tail.

Cont as set, knitting 1 row in each of yarns D, E, F, G and A.

Braid Row Leaving a tail of similar length, join in any braid by knotting it together with the long tail from previous row, knit to end, cut braid leaving a long tail.

Work from ** to ** as given for Mixed Messages runner until cushion measures approx 15in (37cm) from beg.

Knit 7 rows, using only the seven yarns in any order. Using A, bind off loosely.

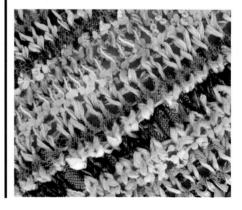

to finish...

Press according to instructions on ball bands. Fold 16in (40cm) up to form a pocket. Sew side seams. Trim the fringe on the top edge of the pocket to 2in (5cm). Insert cushion pad. Fold flap over.

The cushion is worked in an 'envelope' style, so the cushion pad can easily be inserted and removed simply by opening up the flap.

Here we've run riot with both colour and texture to create a unique item that will look dazzling in any room.

DESIGN SECRETS UNRAVELLED...

Choose two or three colours to fit in with your interior; you don't have to use a scheme as bright as this cushion. You could work the cushion in the same yarns and media as the runner, or in softer earth tones. Choose a wider palette of pastels and use printed floral ribbons, lace and daisy braids for a romantic look. Alternatively, work the cushions in rich browns and golds and add metallic trims for a sophisticated autumnal feel.

YARN FOCUS

Although worked in the same way as the Mixed Messages runner, I wanted the cushion to have a totally different look and so chose shiny or synthetic yarns in a palette of three colours: hot pink, turquoise and bright green. Eyelash yarn and ribbon contrast against a smooth silk yarn and a yarn with multi-coloured sequins. The other media were great fun to source; among those I found were a tasselled braid and ricrac braid in very bright green, organza ribbon and a strip of sequins in pink, and a turquoise ribbon with bright yellow spots.

hot pink synthetic

green organza

textured ribbon

sequinned blue

weight

tasselled braid

blue light weight

patchwork pieces

The designs featured in this chapter are knitted in mitred squares. This is a form of patchwork knitting, in which each square or diamond is worked by picking up stitches from those around it. You can create some truly stunning colour effects using this technique, playing with geometric shapes to create either random or structured patterns – as showcased in the Hedgerow Harlequin (pages 52–53). You also achieve rich textures, as some rows are worked in smooth stockinette and some rows in the more bumpy, textural garter stitch – as seen in the Springtime Shades cushion (pages 54–55).

Using mitred squares creates a piece that is full of dramatic colour contrasts and rich texture.

DESIGN SECRETS UNRAVELLED...

You could work this throw in bright summer cottons for sunnier days or in dark, dramatic purple, mauve, plum and aubergine for a stylish bedroom throw. This method of knitting is also ideal for using up all the oddments in your yarn stash; pick out colours and textures at random and use three to each shape or work each shape in one yarn.

YARN FOCUS

I have used 18 different yarns for this throw to create a blaze of autumnal colour. I chose greens, oranges, rusts and golds for the autumn leaves and added shades of purple and red for the hedgerow berries. Most of the yarns are wool or wool mix. I used seven tweed yarns for added texture and a wonderful soft chenille in dusty pale green. Mixed with these are smooth wool yarns in solid colours and two fantastic multi-coloured yarns that vary from browns and rusts through to bright green and pink.

dark green

autumn texture

russet

rust

gold

pale green

rich damson   dark purple

burnt orange   red tweed

autumn tweed

leaf green

hedgerow harlequin

MEASUREMENTS
44in (112cm) square

GATHER TOGETHER...
Materials
2 x 1¾oz (50g) balls of light-weight (DK)
or medium-weight (aran) or bulky-weight
(chunky) yarn in each of the following shades:
5 shades of green ranging from dark to light
3 shades of orange and rust ranging from
dark to light
2 shades of gold and yellow
6 shades of berries ranging from dark red
to purple
2 multi-coloured autumnal shades

Needles
1 pair of size 10½ (7mm) needles

GAUGE
Basic Diamond at widest point: 5½in (14cm)
using size 10½ (7mm) needles

*Knit Note: Use two strands of light-weight
(DK) and medium-weight (aran) yarns together
throughout. Make sure that you work through
all strands for each stitch.*

*Changing colours: Tie the new colour to the
old colour securely and weave in the ends
as you work.*

*Edge stitches: These are always slipped purlwise;
in the instructions this is written 'sl 1wyif'. This
forms a chain of large stitches along the edge,
which makes it easier to pick up stitches. Slip
the last stitch with the yarn at the front of the
work (the side facing you). If the penultimate
stitch is a knit stitch, you will have to bring the
yarn forward between the needles. If it is a purl
stitch, the yarn will be in the correct position.
Always knit the stitch on the return row – the
yarn will be in the knit position to remind you.
This stitch is always included in the total of
stitches to be knitted.*

In this autumn-inspired throw, each shape is worked by picking up stitches
from those around it, so there is no sewing to do. The colours are chosen
at random to create the glorious patchwork effect. The squares are shaped
with the sk2po decrease (see page 109); each one is worked in three colours
in garter stitch and stockinette stitch stripes. The shapes are used on their ends
to form diagonal lines of diamonds. The tassels are added to the zigzag edges
after the main piece has been knitted.

Knit your throw...
Use the colours randomly throughout the throw.
When picking up stitches, pick up knitwise by
inserting the needle from RS of work through to WS
of work under one of the chain sts created on the
edge of a square, wrap the yarn around the needle
and pull a loop through.

Basic Diamond (BD)
Using size 10½ (7mm) needles and any colour,
cast on 25 sts using the cable cast-on method
(see page 103).
Row 1 (WS) K24, sl 1wyif.
Row 2 K11, sk2po, k10, sl 1wyif. 23 sts.
Row 3 K22, sl 1wyif.
Row 4 K10, sk2po, k9, sl 1wyif. 21 sts.
Row 5 K20, sl 1 wyif.

Change colour.
Row 6 K9, sk2po, k8, sl 1wyif. 19 sts.
Row 7 K18, sl 1 wyif.
Row 8 K8, sk2po, k7, sl 1wyif. 17 sts.
Row 9 K the sl st, p15, sl 1wyif.
Row 10 K7, sk2po, k6, sl 1wyif. 15 sts.
Row 11 K the sl st, p13, sl 1wyif.
Row 12 K6, sk2po, k5, sl 1wyif. 13 sts.
Row 13 K12, sl 1wyif.

Change colour.
Row 14 K5, sk2po, k4, sl 1wyif. 11 sts.
Row 15 K10, sl 1wyif.
Row 16 K4, sk2po, k3, sl 1wyif. 9 sts.
Row 17 K8, sl 1wyif.
Row 18 K3, sk2po, k2, sl 1wyif. 7 sts.
Row 19 K6, sl 1wyif.

Row 20 K2, sk2po, k1, sl 1wyif. 5 sts.
Row 21 K4, sl 1wyif.
Row 22 K1, sk2po, sl 1wyif. 3 sts.
Row 23 K2, sl 1wyif.
Row 24 Sk2po. 1 st.
Cut yarn and pull through rem st.

Diamond 1 (D1)
Using size 10½ (7mm) needles and any colour,
cast on 25 sts using the cable cast-on method and
work as given for Basic Diamond.

Diamond 2 (D2)
With RS of work facing and using any colour, pick
up and knit 13 sts down left edge of D1 and 12 sts
up right edge of BD. 25 sts.
Work as given for BD.

Diamond 3 (D3 – Left Edge Diamond)
With RS of work facing and using any colour, pick
up and knit 13 sts down left edge of D2, turn work
and cast on 12 sts using the cable cast-on method.
25 sts.
Work as given for BD.

Diamond 4 (D4)
Using size 10½ (7mm) needles and any colour,
cast on 25 sts using the cable cast-on method and
work as given for BD.

Diamond 5 (D5)
With RS of work facing and using any colour, pick
up and knit 13 sts down left edge of D4 and 12 sts
up right edge of D1. 25 sts.
Work as given for BD.

Diamond 6 (D6)
With RS of work facing and using any colour, pick
up and knit 13 sts down left edge of D5 and 12 sts
up right edge of D2. 25 sts.
Work as given for BD.

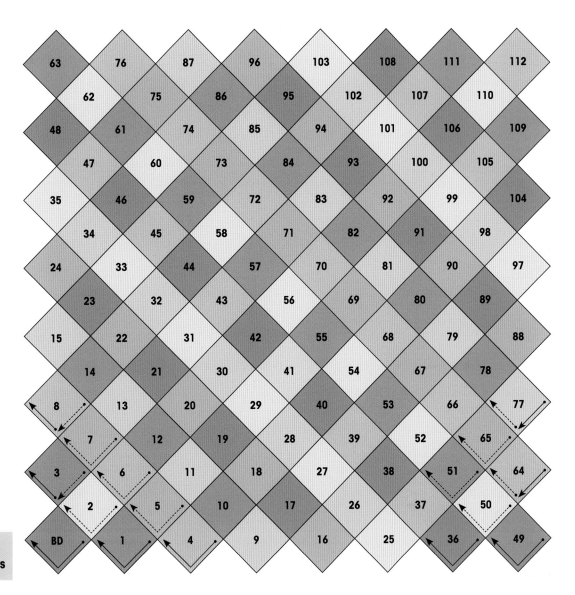

- → **cast-on stitches**
- ⇢ **picked-up stitches**

Diamond 7 (D7)

With RS of work facing and using any colour, pick up and knit 13 sts down left edge of D6 and 12sts up right edge of D3. 25 sts.

Work as given for BD.

Diamond 8 (D8 – Left Edge Diamond)

With RS of work facing and using any colour, pick up and knit 13 sts down left edge of D7, turn work and cast on 12 sts using the cable cast-on method. 25 sts.

Work as given for BD.

Three diagonal rows have now been completed. Referring to the diagram, continue to work in diagonal rows as follows:

Diamonds 9, 16, 25, 36, 49 Cast on 25 sts and work as given for BD.

Diamonds 15, 24, 35, 48, 63 Pick up and cast on sts as given for D3 (Left Edge Diamond).

Continue until row D49 to D63 has been completed.

Diamond 64 (D64 – Right Edge Diamond)

With RS of work facing and using any colour, cast on 12 sts then pick up and knit 13 sts up right edge of D50. 25 sts.

Work as given for BD.

Referring to the diagram, continue to work in diagonal rows as follows:

Diamonds 77, 88, 97, 104, 109 and 112

Cast on and pick up sts as given for D64 (Right Edge Diamond).

To finish...

Press according to instructions on ball bands. Trim all ends neatly.

Tassels

Using several different yarns together, wrap the yarns loosely around a piece of cardboard 7in (18cm) wide several times. Cut the wrapped strands at the bottom and remove the cardboard. Take three lengths of different yarns and fold in half. Using a crochet hook, pull the strands through the tips of the diamonds from front to back by catching the fold with the hook. Pass the ends through the folded loop and pull to tighten the knot. Continue until every diamond tip has a tassel.

springtime shades

The back of the cushion is made in one large mitred square.

This finer, lighter version of the throw is worked in rows of squares to make the front of the cushion. The back is one large version of the basic diamond. A tassel is added to each corner as a finishing flourish.

MEASUREMENTS
12½in (32cm) square

GATHER TOGETHER...
Materials
1 x 1¾oz (50g) ball of light-weight (DK) yarn in nine shades of spring green ranging from dark to light
12½in (32cm) square cushion pad

Needles
1 pair of size 6 (4mm) needles

GAUGE
Basic Diamond at widest point: 3½in (9cm) using size 6 (4mm) needles

DESIGN SECRETS UNRAVELLED...
You could create some fantastic graphic effects using these small squares. Try using only three colours and making each square the same; this will form a three-dimensional square grid. Or you could work squares in the same colours in diagonal lines. Use bright contemporary colours or, for an optical art-inspired fabric, use black, grey and white.

YARN FOCUS
While the throw is inspired by the fiery shades of autumn, this cushion uses colours taken straight from the first spring leaves. I have used nine shades of fresh green, ranging from golden olive through to pale apple green and dusty blue-green. There is also a range of textures: smooth bamboo yarns, soft tape, a tweed of pale lime, a multi-coloured viscose to add a gleam, and a marled yarn for the blue-green of lavender.

Knit your cushion...
Use the colours randomly throughout the cushion.

Front
Basic Diamond (BD)
Using size 6 (4mm) needles and any colour, cast on 25 sts using the cable cast-on method. Work as given for BD of Hedgerow Harlequin.

Diamond 1 (D1)
With RS of work facing and using any colour, pick up and knit 13 sts down left edge of BD, turn work and cast on 12 sts using the cable cast-on method. 25 sts.
Work as given for BD.

Diamond 2 (D2)
With RS of work facing and using any colour, pick up and knit 13 sts down left edge of D1, turn work and cast on 12 sts using the cable cast-on method. 25 sts.

Work as given for BD.

Diamond 3 (D3)
With RS of work facing and using any colour, pick up and knit 13 sts down left edge of D2, turn work and cast on 12 sts using the cable cast-on method. 25 sts.
Work as given for BD.

Diamond 4 (D4)
With RS of work facing and using any colour, pick up and knit 13 sts down left edge of D3, turn work and cast on 12 sts using the cable cast-on method. 25 sts.
Work as given for BD.

One row of diamonds has been completed.

dark olive wool
pale lime tweed
apple bamboo
blue-green cotton
pale apple green

4	9	14	19	24
3	8	13	18	23
2	7	12	17	22
1	6	11	16	21
BD	5	10	15	20

→ **cast-on stitches**
⇢ **picked-up stitches**

Diamond 5 (D5 – Lower Edge Diamond)

With RS of work facing and using any colour, cast on 12 sts then pick up and knit 13 sts up right edge of BD. 25 sts. Work as given for BD.

Diamond 6 (D6)

With RS of work facing and using any colour, pick up and knit 13 sts down left edge of D5 and 12 sts up right edge of D1. 25 sts.
Work as given for BD.

Diamonds 7, 8 and 9

Work as given for D6, picking up sts down edge of diamond just worked and up edge of diamond from previous row.

Referring to the diagram, continue to work in rows as follows:
Diamonds 10, 15 and 20 Work as given for D5.
Diamonds 11–14, 16–19, and 21–24 Work as given for D6.

Back

Using size 6 (4mm) needles and any colour, cast on 121 sts.
Row 1 (WS) K120, sl 1wyif.
Row 2 K59, sk2po, k58, sl 1wyif. 119 sts.
Row 3 K118, sl 1wyif.
Row 4 K58, sk2po, k57, sl 1wyif. 117 sts.
Row 5 K116, sl 1 wyif.

Change colour.
Row 6 K57, sk2po, k56, sl 1wyif. 115 sts.
Row 7 K114, sl 1 wyif.
Row 8 K56, sk2po, k55, sl 1wyif. 113 sts.
Row 9 K the sl st, p111, sl 1wyif.
Row 10 K55, sk2po, k54, sl 1wyif. 111 sts.
Row 11 K the sl st, p109, sl 1wyif.
Row 12 K54, sk2po, k53, sl 1wyif. 109 sts.
Row 13 K108, sl 1wyif.

Change colour.
Row 14 K53, sk2po, k52, sl 1wyif. 107 sts.
Row 15 K106, sl 1wyif.
Row 16 K52, sk2po, k51, sl 1wyif. 105 sts.
Row 17 K104, sl 1wyif.
Row 18 K51, sk2po, k50, sl 1wyif. 103 sts.

Row 19 K102, sl 1wyif.
Row 20 K50, sk2po, k49, sl 1wyif. 101 sts.
Row 21 K100, sl 1wyif.
Row 22 K49, sk2po, k48, sl 1wyif. 99 sts.
Row 23 K98, sl 1wyif.

**Change colour.
Row 24 K to centre 3 sts, sk2po, k to last st, sl 1wyif.
Row 25 K to last st, sl 1wyif.
Rep rows 24 and 25 twice more.

Change colour.
Row 30 K to centre 3 sts, sk2po, k to last st, sl 1wyif.
Row 31 K to last st, sl 1wyif.
Row 32 As row 30.
Row 33 K the sl st, p to last st, sl 1wyif.
Rep rows 32 and 33 once more.
Rep rows 30 and 31 once more.

Change colour.
Row 38 K to centre 3 sts, sk2po, k to last st, sl 1wyif.
Row 39 K to last st, sl 1wyif.
Rep rows 38 and 39 4 times more.**
Rep from ** to ** until 3 sts remain.
Next Row Sk2po.
Cut yarn and pull through rem st.

To finish…

Press according to instructions on ball bands. Trim all ends neatly. Sew front to back around three sides, making sure the large diamond on the back points in the same direction as the small diamonds on the front and matching g st and st st stripes. Insert cushion pad. Sew rem edge closed. Using all yarns together, make a tassel for each corner as given for Hedgerow Harlequin.

cubist colours

For the projects in this chapter, I wanted to focus on high-impact graphic styles, to make a feature of the shapes of the seating cube and the square cushion. Working with square motifs knitted in bold stripes makes a strong visual statement, whether you feature lots of colours, as in the gloriously vibrant, fluorescently bright seating cube shown here, or just two simple contrasting colours, as in the utterly chic black and white cushion shown on pages 60–61. Both of these projects are knitted using double-pointed and circular needles.

The square motif is knitted from the centre outwards. You'll start the work on double-pointed needles, and then, as the work grows, transfer the knitting onto a circular needle.

DESIGN SECRETS UNRAVELLED...

Use the multi-yarn ball technique to knit stripes to complement your décor. Choose cool greens for the garden or sea shades for a holiday home. Use soft pastels for a bedroom or dramatic darks for a study. Use the cube as a seat, a footstool, put a tray on top for a coffee table or use as a bedside table.

YARN FOCUS

For this project I chose the brightest and funkiest colours in the yarn shop: fluorescent and day-glo shades of orange, lemon and lime with a splash of pink. Add to this mix metallic gold and orange and the cube is perfect for a modern interior or a teenager's room. I've used light-weight (DK) cotton yarns to make the seat hard-wearing, using two strands together so it knits up quickly. Make up a multi-yarn ball so there's no need to worry about counting rounds for the stripes. I started the sequence with lemon and gold, then bright tangerine, pale lime, lipstick pink, burnt orange with hot orange metallic, then bright lime, acid yellow, dark orange and hot pink.

lipstick pink

pale lime green

acid yellow

bright pink

orange

bright lime

tangerine

lemon yellow

citrus squares

MEASUREMENTS
18in (45cm) square and 18in (45cm) deep

GATHER TOGETHER...
Materials
1 x 1¾oz (50g) ball of light-weight (DK) cotton (92yd/84m per ball) in lemon plus 2 x ⅞oz (25g) balls of light-weight (4ply) metallic yarn (110yd/100m per ball) in gold (**A**)

2 x 1¾oz (50g) balls of light-weight (DK) cotton (93yd/85m per ball) in each of tangerine (**B**), acid yellow (**G**) and dark orange (**H**)

2 x 1¾oz (50g) balls of light-weight (DK) wool/cotton yarn (123yd/113m per ball) in pale lime (**C**)

2 x 1¾oz (50g) balls of fine-weight (4ply) mercerized cotton (186yd/170m per ball) in lipstick pink (**D**)

2 x 1¾oz (50g) balls of light-weight (DK) cotton (92yd/84m per ball) in burnt orange plus 2 x ⅞oz (25g) balls of light-weight (4ply) metallic yarn (110yd/100m per ball) in orange (**E**)

1 x 3½oz (100g) hank of medium-weight (aran) cotton (150yd/137m per hank) in bright lime (**F**)

1 x 3½oz (100g) ball of light-weight (DK) mercerized cotton (230yd/210m per ball) in bright pink (**I**)

Cube of seating foam 18in (45cm) x 18in (45cm) x 18in (45cm) or fabric cube of same measurements filled with polystyrene balls (bean-bag filler)

Needles
1 set of size 10½ (7mm) double-pointed needles
1 size 10½ (7mm) 31in (80cm)-long circular needle

GAUGE
15 sts and 19 rows to 4in (10cm) measured over st st (1 row k, 1 row p) using size 10½ (7mm) needles

Knit Note: *Because you are using a multi-yarn ball with lots of ends, weave them in as you knit to save time sewing them in later.*

The top of this seating cube is a square motif, worked from the centre outwards on double-pointed needles. The sides are picked up around the square and knitted on circular needles. The stripes are worked randomly, using a multi-yarn ball, so it's easy to just cast on and knit. The base is not knitted but made out of hard-wearing fabric to resist wear and tear.

Prepare your project...
Yarns A and E: use one strand of light-weight (DK) yarn together with two strands of fine-weight (4ply) metallic yarn throughout.

Yarns B, C, G, H and I: use two strands of light-weight (DK) yarn throughout.

Yarn D: use three strands of fine-weight (4ply) yarn throughout.

Yarn F: use one strand of medium-weight (aran) yarn throughout.

Lay out the yarns in sequence from A to I, having divided the balls into the correct number of strands. Beginning with A (cotton yarn plus metallic yarn), pull out 3 arm's lengths and wind it into a ball. Tie on B, leaving 2in (5cm) ends (these are woven in during knitting). Pull out 6 arm's lengths and continue winding onto the ball. Tie on C, pull out 6 arm's lengths and wind it onto the ball. Continue tying on the next yarn in the sequence as follows:

D and E: 8 lengths
F and G: 10 lengths
H and I: 12 lengths
A and B: 16 lengths
C and D: 20 lengths
E and F: 22 lengths
G and H: 24 lengths
I: 26 lengths

Rewind the ball so A is at the beginning ready to knit with first.

Knit your seating cube cover...
Top
Using size 10½ (7mm) double-pointed needles, cast on 8 sts, arranging 2 sts on each of four needles.

Round 1 K8. Place a marker to show end of round, slip this marker on every round.

Round 2 (Kf&b) into each st. 16 sts.

Round 3 and every foll alt row K to end.

Round 4 *(Kf&b) into next st, k2, (kf&b) into next st; rep from * three times more. 24 sts.

Round 6 *(Kf&b) into next st, k4, (kf&b) into next st; rep from * three times more. 32 sts.

Round 8 *(Kf&b) into next st, k6, (kf&b) into next st; rep from * three times more. 40 sts.

Round 10 *(Kf&b) into next st, k8, (kf&b) into next st; rep from * three times more. 48 sts.

Round 12 *(Kf&b) into next st, k10, (kf&b) into next st; rep from * three times more. 24 sts.

Don't hold back: vibrant, clashing colours will have the greatest impact for this project.

your yarn, your style!

Rework this cube in shades inspired by a flower garden: soft pink, lilac, leaf green and cream. Add flower buttons for a pretty touch. Or use shades of blue, aqua and sea green highlighted with natural shell buttons. Sew the buttons onto the sides where colours change for added texture.

Cont in this way, working 2 sts more between incs on every alt row and transferring to the circular needle when you have sufficient sts. Cont until there are 50 sts on each side of the square, ending with an inc row. Square should measure approx 9½in (24cm) from centre.
Bind off very loosely.

Sides
Make up a ball as above, beginning with the same yarn used for the last stripe on the top, in the sequence of lengths: 26, 28, 24, 30 and 22. Repeat until you have made up a grapefruit-sized ball. Rewind the ball so the first yarn is at the beginning. Make up more yarn as you need it, keeping colour sequence correct.

With RS of work facing and using size 10½ (7mm) circular needles, pick up and k 50 sts along each side of square. 200 sts.
Knit every rnd until sides measure 18in (45cm) from beg.
Bind off loosely.

to finish...
Press according to instructions on ball bands.

Foam insert
Cover the foam with a fabric slip cover, using a hard-wearing canvas or fake suede fabric for the base (see pages 118–119 for covering cushions). Pull the knitted cover onto foam insert, matching corners and seams on the top. Pin the knitted fabric onto the foam, pulling so the sides are completely covered. Using strong sewing thread, sew the knitted fabric to the base fabric.

IN THE MIX
Yarns include cream wool bouclé, leaf green cotton, soft gold tape, baby pink mohair and lilac mercerized cotton. Decorate with daisy-shaped shell buttons in soft pink, cream and cornflower blue.

IN THE MIX
Yarns include blue silk/cotton tweed, light aqua bamboo, sea-green and aqua metallics, storm-blue cotton and pale aqua fleece. Decorate with natural shell buttons.

black and white blocks

MEASUREMENTS
16in (40cm) square

GATHER TOGETHER...
Materials
2 x 3½oz (100g) balls of super-bulky
(super-chunky) wool yarn (87yd/80m per ball)
in each of white (**A**) and black (**B**)

16in (40cm) square cushion pad

Needles
1 set of size 11 (8mm) double-pointed needles
1 size 11 (8mm) 24in (60cm)-long
circular needles

GAUGE
12 sts and 16 rows to 4in (10cm) measured
over st st (1 row k, 1 row p) using
size 11 (8mm) needles

Black and white never goes out of style, and this simple cushion will make a strong style impact on any room. The cushion is made from two square motifs worked in a graphic stripe pattern. Worked in thick yarn, this project is ideal as an introduction to knitting on double-pointed needles.

Knit your cushion...
Back and Front
(Make 2)
Using size 11 (8mm) double-pointed needles and A, cast on 8 sts, arranging 2 sts on each of four needles.
Round 1 Using A, k8. Place a marker to show end of round, slip this marker on every round.
Round 2 Using A, (kf&b) into each st. 16 sts.
Round 3 Using B, k to end.
Round 4 Using B, *(kf&b) into next st, k2, (kf&b) into next st; rep from * three times more. 24 sts.
Round 5 Using B, k to end.
Round 6 Using B, *(kf&b) into next st, k4, (kf&b) into next st; rep from * three times more. 32 sts.
Round 7 Using A, k to end.
Round 8 Using A, *(kf&b) into next st, k6, (kf&b) into next st; rep from * three times more. 40 sts.
Round 9 Using A, k to end.
Round 10 Using A, *(kf&b) into next st, k8, (kf&b) into next st; rep from * three times more. 48 sts.
Working in stripes of 4 rows B and 4 rows A, cont in this way, working 2 sts more between incs on every alt row and transferring to the circular needle when you have sufficient sts. Cont until square measures approx 8in (20.5cm) from centre, ending with 4th row of stripe.
Bind off loosely.

to finish...
Sew in all ends neatly. Press according to instructions on ball bands. Sew back and front together around three sides. Insert cushion pad. Sew rem side closed.

DESIGN SECRETS UNRAVELLED...
Use two contrasting colours; funky hot pink and green, or stylish chocolate and cream. Use toning colours like aqua and sea green for a cool summer cushion or, for winter, choose warm shades like pumpkin and rust. Have a different colour for each stripe, using up your yarn stash, making a thick yarn by combining several strands together.

chunky white wool

chunky black wool

YARN FOCUS
Really thick yarns are great to work with, producing huge stitches and, of course, quick results. This is a wool yarn in black and white that graphically shows the way the motif is worked.

life's a beach

A breaking wave inspired this beach throw, with the variegated blue yarn suggesting the colours of the ocean and the sand, and the white yarn worked in a special loop stitch to resemble the froth of surf on waves. The matching cushion also features the wonderfully textural loop stitch. The yarns used are sturdy and robust enough to make items resilient enough to be used outside – ideal for summer beach picnics. Alternatively, these items will introduce a lively seaside atmosphere into any interior, and the chunky wool yarns used for both projects will add warmth and cosiness.

This thick-and-thin yarn knits up into a fascinating slubby, organic-looking fabric, while the variegated colours merge and mingle to create a beautiful pattern.

YARN FOCUS

This multi-coloured thick-and-thin yarn made the perfect material for this ocean-inspired throw. The colours are reminiscent of a sandy beach, with turquoise, blue and shell. The 'wave' is made in a pure white yarn of similar thickness that creates thick loops for maximum texture.

DESIGN SECRETS UNRAVELLED...

It would be easy to make up your own yarn for this throw. Collect together a range of sea-inspired yarns such as textured cottons and shiny viscose, adding different textures such as slubs and bouclés into the mix. Knit a sample using several yarns together to obtain an equivalent to the super-bulky weight I used; you might need to add or subtract yarns until you achieve the correct gauge. Choose shades of blue to reflect a Caribbean sea – deep turquoises and jewel blues – or go for cooler aquas and sea greens for northern seas. It is easier to work the loop stitch using one strand, but every super-bulky yarn range features a shade of white so this should be easy to source.

surf-inspired

sand and sea

wool

chunky white wool

breaking waves

MEASUREMENTS
59in (150cm) square

GATHER TOGETHER...
Materials
A 15 x 3½oz (100g) balls of super-bulky-weight thick-and-thin wool yarn (54yd/50m per ball) in multi-coloured sea colours

B 3 x 3½oz (100g) balls of super-bulky-weight wool yarn (87yd/80m per ball) in white

Needles
1 size 17 (12mm) 40in (100cm)-long circular needle

GAUGE
8 sts and 11 rows to 4in (10cm) square measured over st st (1 row k, 1 row p) using size 17 (12mm) circular needle

SPECIAL ABBREVIATIONS
Loop st Work each loop twice around finger for long loop (see page 107)

Kf&b Work knitwise on knit rows and purlwise on p rows (see page 108)

Knit Note: The circular needle is used to accommodate the large number of sts, not for circular knitting. Turn work after every row.

This stockinette stitch square throw is worked from corner to corner, so the fantastic sea-inspired yarn appears in diagonal waves. The throw is shaped using kf&b and yon to increase, then ssk and ssp, and k2tog and p2tog to decrease. The corner is worked in frothy loop stitch in a pure white yarn.

Knit your throw...
Using size 17 (12mm) circular needle and A, cast on 3 sts.
**Foundation Row Yon, k2, kf&b. 5 sts.

Commence shaping
Row 1 Yon, p to last st, kf&b.
Row 2 Yon, k to last st, kf&b.
Row 3 Yon, p to last st, kf&b.
Row 4 Yon, k to last st, kf&b.
Row 5 Yon, p to end.
Row 6 Yon, k to end.***
Rep these 6 rows until straight edge from point to needle measures approx 59in (150cm), ending with row 6. 175 sts.
Next Row P to end.
Next Row K to end.

Commence shaping
Row 1 Ssp, p to last 2 sts, p2tog.
Row 2 K2tog, k to last 2 sts, ssk.
Row 3 Ssp, p to last 2 sts, p2tog.
Row 4 K2tog, k to last 2 sts, ssk.
Row 5 Ssp, p to end.
Row 6 K2tog, k to end.
Rep these 6 rows until straight edge from point

to needle measures approx 29½in (75cm), ending with row 6. 95 sts.
Change to yarn B and commence loop stitch.
****Row 1 Ssp, p to last 2 sts, p2tog.
Row 2 K2tog, k to last 2 sts, ssk.
Row 3 Ssp, loop st, *k1, loop st; rep from * to last 2 sts, p2tog.
Row 4 K2tog, (k1tbl) into each st to last 2 sts, ssk.
Row 5 Ssp, p to end.
Row 6 K2tog, k to end.
Row 7 Ssp, loop st, *k1, loop st; rep from * to last 2 sts, p2tog.
Row 8 K2tog, (k1tbl) into each st to last 2 sts, ssk.
Row 9 Ssp, p to last 2 sts, p2tog.
Row 10 K2tog, k to last 2 sts, ssk.
Row 11 Ssp, loop st, *k1, loop st; rep from * to last 2 sts, p2.
Row 12 K2tog, (k1tbl) into each st to end.*****
Rep these 12 rows to 5 sts, ending with row 6.
Next Row Ssp, loop st, p2tog. 3 sts.
Bind off.

to finish...
Sew in all ends neatly. Pin out into a square to finished measurements and press according to instructions on ball bands.

MEASUREMENTS

16in (40cm) square

Materials

3 x 3½oz (100g) balls of super-bulky-weight
wool yarn (87yd/80m per ball) in white

16in (40cm) cushion pad

Needles

1 pair of size 17 (12mm) needles

GAUGE

8 sts and 11 rows to 4in (10cm)
square measured over st st (1 row k, 1 row p)
using size 17 (12mm) needles

SPECIAL ABBREVIATION

Loop st Work each loop twice around finger
for long loop (see page 107)

chunky white wool

chunky white wool

YARN FOCUS

The cushion is knitted in the same
yarn that I used for the corner of the
Breaking Waves throw, so that they
could be used together to form
a co-ordinating set. The yarn is
a wonderfully soft wool made
with a loose single twist.

This matching cushion is made in the same way as the throw; it is knitted
in a square, worked diagonally from corner to corner. Just the white yarn
is used this time, and the corner section of loop stitch is featured again
to complement the throw.

Knit your cushion...

Front

Using size 17 (12mm) circular needle, cast on
3 sts.
Work as given for the Breaking Waves throw from **
to ***. 15 sts.
Rep these 6 rows until straight edge from point
to needle measures approx 16in (40cm), ending
with row 6. 45 sts.
Next Row P to end.
Next Row K to end.
Work as given for Breaking Waves throw from ****
to *****.
Rep these 12 rows to 5 sts, ending with row 12.
Next Row Ssp, p1, p2tog. 3 sts.
Bind off.

Back

Using size 17 (12mm) circular needle, cast on
3 sts.
Work as given for Breaking Waves throw from **
to ***. 15 sts.
Rep these 6 rows until straight edge from point to
needle measures approx 16in (40cm), ending with
row 6. 45 sts.
Next Row P to end.
Next Row K to end.
Commence shaping
Row 1 Ssp, p to last 2 sts, p2tog.
Row 2 K2tog, k to last 2 sts, ssk.
Row 3 Ssp, p to last 2 sts, p2tog.
Row 4 K2tog, k to last 2 sts, ssk.
Row 5 Ssp, p to end.
Row 6 K2tog, k to end.
Rep these 6 rows to 5 sts, ending with row 6.
Next Row Ssp, p1, p2tog. 3 sts.
Bind off.

to finish...

Sew in all ends neatly. Pin out into a square
to finished measurements and press according
to instructions on ball bands. Join back and front
together around three sides. Insert cushion pad
and sew remaining side closed.

*The loop stitch creates a fabric with a
fantastically deep, plush pile.*

rustic entrelac

Entrelac is a technique for patchwork
knitting. This method is usually worked
in smaller squares, but for this project
I chose a bulky-weight (chunky) yarn.
I wanted to experiment by changing the
scale of the entrelac, creating large, bold
squares suitable for the size of this throw.
I used two glowing autumnal colours
in flecked tweed yarn; a basketweave
effect is created as the different textures
weave around each other. Four different
stitch patterns are used for the panels
of the throw, so it would still look stunning
and full of interest even if it were made
in a single colour.

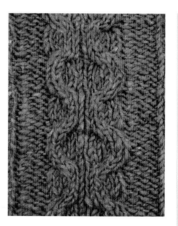

*The entrelac throw is made
up of four types of knitted panel;
one in stockinette, one in moss
stitch (which non-US knitters
call double moss stitch), one
in a lace pattern, and one in
a cable pattern (shown above).*

DESIGN SECRETS UNRAVELLED...

You could use four colours for this
throw, one for each texture; just join
in a new colour to begin a new square.
As well as thick wools, try chenille
in damson and berry for super-cosy
luxury. Change the look for spring
and summer by working the squares
in heavy cottons in the colours of
spring flowers or blowsy summer
roses. Choose two shades of one
colour; light turquoise and aqua blue
for the beach, or vibrant raspberry
and rose for a bedroom.

YARN FOCUS

I have always loved tweed wool yarns
for autumn and winter; I know they're
going to be warm just by looking at
them. The tweed texture adds depth and
unexpected dots of colour to the fabric.
I chose this bulky-weight (chunky) yarn
for warmth, while the glowing gold
together with a fiery rust reflect the
rich colours of autumn.

gold wool tweed

rus

gold wool tweed

rust wool tweed

rustic entrelac

Entrelac is a type of patchwork knitting where stitches are picked up or worked together to join the squares; there is no sewing together. There are four fabrics used for the squares: stockinette stitch and moss stitch are worked alternately for one row of squares in a glowing golden yarn, and a simple lace pattern and cable design in a warm rust colour make up the two squares on the next row.

MEASUREMENTS

62in (158cm) square

GATHER TOGETHER...
Materials

A 9 x 3½oz (100g) balls of bulky-weight (chunky) wool tweed yarn (109yd/100m per ball) in gold
B 9 x 3½oz (100g) balls of bulky-weight (chunky) wool tweed yarn (109yd/100m per ball) in rust

Needles and notions

1 size 10½ (7mm) 40in (100cm)-long circular needle
Cable needle
Stitch markers

GAUGE

12 sts and 18 rows to 4in (10cm) measured over stockinette stitch (1 row k, 1 row p) using size 10½ (7mm) circular needle and A

SPECIAL ABBREVIATIONS

C4B Cable 4 back by slipping the next 2 sts on to a cable needle at back of work, k2, then k2 sts from cable needle.
C4F Cable 4 front by slipping the next 2 sts on to a cable needle at front of work, k2, then k2 sts from cable needle.

Knit Note:
The pattern instructions refer to moss stitch. This is a US term; non-US knitters know this stitch as double moss stitch.

Knit Note:
Refer to the diagram on page 73 before you start knitting.

Knit Notes:

Edge stitches: These are always slipped purlwise; in the instructions this is written 'sl 1wyif'. This forms a chain of large stitches along the edge, which makes it easier to pick up stitches. Whatever the texture you are working, slip the last stitch with the yarn at the front of the work (the side facing you). If the penultimate stitch is a knit stitch, you will have to bring the yarn forward between the needles. If it is a purl stitch, the yarn will be in the correct position. Knit the stitch on the return row; the yarn will be in the knit position to remind you.

Picking up stitches: This is done either knitwise with the right side of the fabric facing you or purlwise with the wrong side facing. Pick up knitwise by inserting the needle from RS of work through to WS of work under one of the chain sts created on the edge of a square as described above, wrap the yarn around the needle and pull a loop through. Pick up purlwise by inserting the needle from RS to WS and pulling a loop through. Knitwise the needle goes away from you and purlwise the needle comes towards you.

Circular needle: The circular needle is only used to hold the large number of stitches and hold the weight of the throw as you add more squares. You use it like a pair of ordinary needles by turning at the end of every row.

Row instructions: Each written row is actually two rows, a RS row followed by a WS row (sometimes the WS row comes first). Follow the instructions carefully and turn the work when told to work the return row.

Knit your throw...

Begin with a foundation line of four triangles worked alternately in short rows of st st and moss stitch.
Using size 10½ (7mm) circular needle and A, cast on 108 sts loosely, placing a marker after every 27 sts.

Triangle 1

Using A, over the first 27 cast-on sts work a st st triangle as follows:
Row 1 K2 and turn, p1, sl 1wyif and turn. 2 sts.
Row 2 K the sl st, k2 (triangle st and next cast-on st), turn, p2, sl 1wyif, turn. 3 sts.
Row 3 K the sl st, k3 (triangle sts and next cast-on st), turn, p3, sl 1wyif, turn. 4 sts.
Row 4 K the sl st, k4 (triangle sts and next cast-on st), turn, p4, sl 1wyif, turn. 5 sts.
Row 5 K the sl st, k5 (triangle sts and next cast-on st), turn, p5, sl 1wyif, turn. 6 sts.
Continue in this way, working 1 more cast-on st on the RS of each row until the following row has been worked:
Row 25 K the sl st, k25 (triangle sts and next cast-on st), turn, p25, sl 1wyif, turn.
Last Row K the sl st, k26 (triangle sts and next cast-on st), DO NOT TURN. 27 sts.

Triangle 2

Using A, over the next 27 cast-on sts work a moss st triangle as follows:

Row 1 K2, turn, p1, sl 1wyif, turn. 2 sts.
Row 2 K the sl st, k2 (triangle st and next cast-on st), turn, p2, sl 1wyif, turn. 3 sts.
From now on, 1 more cast-on st is worked on RS of each row.
Row 3 K the sl st, p1, k2, turn, p2, k1, sl 1wyif, turn. 4 sts.
Row 4 K the sl st, k1, p1, k2, turn, p2, k1, p1, sl 1wyif, turn. 5 sts.
Row 5 K the sl st, p1, k1, p1, k2, turn, p2, k1, p1, k1, sl 1wyif, turn. 6 sts.
Row 6 K the sl st, (k1, p1) twice, k2, turn, p2, k1, p1, k1, p2, sl 1wyif, turn. 7 sts.
Row 7 K the sl st, (p1, k1) twice, p1, k2, turn, p2, (k1, p1) twice, k1, sl 1wyif, turn. 8 sts.
Row 8 K the sl st, (k1, p1) 3 times, k2, turn, p2, (k1, p1) 3 times, sl 1wyif, turn. 9 sts.
Row 9 K the sl st, (p1, k1) 3 times, p1, k2, turn, p2, (k1, p1) 3 times, k1, sl 1wyif, turn. 10 sts.
Row 10 K the sl st, (k1, p1) 4 times, k2, turn, p2, (k1, p1) 4 times, sl 1wyif, turn. 11 sts.
Row 11 K the sl st, (p1, k1) 4 times, p1, k2, turn, p2, (k1, p1) 4 times, k1, sl 1wyif, turn. 12 sts.
Row 12 K the sl st, (k1, p1) 5 times, k2, turn, p2, (k1, p1) 5 times, sl 1wyif, turn. 13 sts.
Row 13 K the sl st, (p1, k1) 5 times, p1, k2, turn, p2, (k1, p1) 5 times, k1, sl 1wyif, turn. 14 sts.
Row 14 K the sl st, (k1, p1) 6 times, k2, turn, p2, (k1, p1) 6 times, sl 1wyif, turn. 15 sts.
Row 15 K the sl st, (p1, k1) 6 times, p1, k2, turn, p2, (k1, p1) 6 times, k1, sl 1wyif, turn. 16 sts.
Row 16 K the sl st, (k1, p1) 7 times, k2, turn, p2, (k1, p1) 7 times, sl 1wyif, turn. 17 sts.
Row 17 K the sl st, (p1, k1) 7 times, p1, k2, turn, p2, (k1, p1) 7 times, k1, sl 1wyif, turn. 18 sts.
Row 18 K the sl st, (k1, p1) 8 times, k2, turn, p2, (k1, p1) 8 times, sl 1wyif, turn. 19 sts.
Row 19 K the sl st, (p1, k1) 9 times, p1, k2, turn, p2, (k1, p1) 8 times, k1, sl 1wyif, turn. 20 sts.
Row 20 K the sl st, (k1, p1) 9 times, k2, turn, p2, (k1, p1) 9 times, sl 1wyif, turn. 21 sts.

Row 21 K the sl st, (p1, k1) 9 times, p1, k2, turn, p2, (k1, p1) 9 times, k1, sl 1wyif, turn. 22 sts.
Row 22 K the sl st, (k1, p1) 10 times, k2, turn, p2, (k1, p1) 10 times, sl 1wyif, turn. 23 sts.
Row 23 K the sl st, (p1, k1) 10 times, p1, k2, turn, p2, (k1, p1) 10 times, k1, sl 1wyif, turn. 24 sts.
Row 24 K the sl st, (k1, p1) 11 times, k2, turn, p2, (k1, p1) 11 times, sl 1wyif, turn. 25 sts.
Row 25 K the sl st, (p1, k1) 11 times, p1, k2, turn, p2, (k1, p1) 11 times, k1, sl 1wyif, turn. 26 sts.
Row 26 K the sl st, k26 (triangle sts and next cast-on st), DO NOT TURN. 27 sts.

Triangle 3

Using A, over the next 27 cast-on sts work a st st triangle as given for Triangle 1.

Triangle 4

Using A, over the last 27 cast-on sts work a moss st triangle as given for Triangle 2, turning the work at the end of row 26 ready for the next line of squares. Cut yarn A.

****Using B, work a line of three squares worked alternately in lace and cable with two lace triangles at each side to keep the sides of the throw straight as follows:

Triangle 5 worked at the side edge (lace patt – increases from 2 sts to 27 sts).
Row 1 Using B, p2, turn, k2, turn. 2 sts worked in B.
Row 2 Pf&b (shapes the side edge on this and every following row), p2tog (last st of this triangle and next st of Triangle 4 held on needle to join pieces together), turn, k3, turn. 3 sts worked in B.
Row 3 Pf&b, p1, p2tog (last st of this triangle and next st of Triangle 4 held on needle to join pieces together), turn, k4, turn. 4 sts.
Row 4 Pf&b, p2, p2tog (to join pieces as before on this and every following row), turn, k5, turn. 5 sts.
Row 5 Pf&b, p3, p2tog, turn, k6, turn. 6 sts.
Row 6 Pf&b, p4, p2tog, turn, k7, turn. 7 sts.
Row 7 Pf&b, p5, p2tog, turn, k8, turn. 8 sts.
Row 8 Pf&b, p6, p2tog, turn, k9, turn. 9 sts.
Row 9 Pf&b, p7, p2tog, turn, k3, yfwd, ssk, k5, turn. 10 sts.
Row 10 Pf&b, p8, p2tog, turn, k1, k2tog, yfwd, k1, yfwd, ssk, k5, turn. 11 sts.
Row 11 Pf&b, p9, p2tog, turn, k3, yfwd, ssk, k7, turn. 12 sts.
Row 12 Pf&b, p10, p2tog, turn, k13, turn. 13 sts.
Row 13 Pf&b, p11, p2tog, turn, k8, yfwd, ssk, k4, turn. 14 sts.
Row 14 Pf&b, p12, p2tog, turn, k6, k2tog, yfwd, k1,

yfwd, ssk, k4, turn. 15 sts.
Row 15 Pf&b, p13, p2tog, turn, k8, yfwd, ssk, k6, turn. 16 sts.
Row 16 Pf&b, p14, p2tog, turn, k17, turn. 17 sts.
Row 17 Pf&b, p15, p2tog, turn, k3, yfwd, ssk, k8, yfwd, ssk, k3, turn. 18 sts.
Row 18 Pf&b, p16, p2tog, turn, k1, k2tog, yfwd, k1, yfwd, ssk, k5, k2tog, yfwd, k1, yfwd, ssk, k3, turn. 19 sts.
Row 19 Pf&b, p17, p2tog, turn, k3, yfwd, ssk, k8, yfwd, ssk, k5, turn. 20 sts.
Row 20 Pf&b, p18, p2tog, turn, k21, turn. 21 sts.
Row 21 Pf&b, p19, p2tog, turn, (k8, yfwd, ssk) twice, k2, turn. 22 sts.
Row 22 Pf&b, p20, p2tog, turn, k1, (k5, k2tog, yfwd, k1, yfwd, ssk) twice, k2, turn. 23 sts.
Row 23 Pf&b, p21, p2tog, turn, (k8, yfwd, ssk) twice, k4, turn. 24 sts.
Row 24 Pf&b, p22, p2tog, turn, k25, turn. 25 sts.
Row 25 Pf&b, p23, p2tog, turn, k26, turn. 26 sts.
Row 26 Pf&b, p24, p2tog (last st of this triangle and last st of Triangle 4 held on needle to join pieces together), DO NOT TURN. 27 sts.

Square 1

(Cable patt – worked on 27 sts throughout)
Using B and with WS of work facing, pick up 27 sts purlwise along the next edge of Triangle 4, turn.
Row 1 K6, p3, k9, p3, k5, sl 1wyif, turn, k the sl st, p5, k3, p9, k3, p5, p2tog (last st of this square and next st of Triangle 3 held on needle to join pieces together), turn.
**Row 2 As row 1.
Row 3 As row 1.
Row 4 K6, p3, C4B, k1, C4F, p3, k5, sl 1wyif, turn, k the sl st, p5, k3, p9, k3, p5, p2tog (last st of this square and next st of Triangle 3 held on needle), turn.
Row 5 As row 1.
Row 6 As row 1.
Row 7 K6, p3, C4F, k1, C4B, p3, k5, sl 1wyif, turn, k the sl st, p5, k3, p9, k3, p5, p2tog (last st of this square and next st of Triangle 3 held on needle), turn.**

Rep from ** to ** 3 times more.

Row 26 As row 1.

Row 27 K6, p3, k9, p3, k5, sl 1wyif, turn, k the sl st, p5, k3, p9, k3, p5, p2tog (last st of this square and last st of Triangle 3 held on needle), DO NOT TURN.

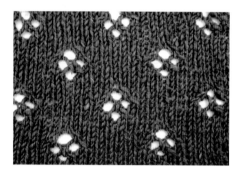

Square 2

(Lace patt – worked on 27 sts throughout)

Using B and with WS of work facing, pick up 27 sts purlwise along the next edge of Triangle 3, turn.

Row 1 K26, sl 1wyif, turn, k the sl st, p25, p2tog (last st of this square and next st of Triangle 2 held on needle to join the pieces together), turn.

**Row 2 As row 1.

Row 3 K3, yfwd, ssk, (k8, yfwd, ssk) twice, k1, sl 1wyif, turn, k the sl st, p25, p2tog (last st of this triangle and next st of Triangle 2 held on needle to join the pieces together), turn.

Row 4 K1, k2tog, yfwd, k1, yfwd, ssk, (k5, k2tog, yfwd, k1, yfwd, ssk) twice, sl 1wyif, turn, k the sl st, p25, p2tog (last st of this square and next st of Triangle 2 held on needle), turn.

Row 5 As row 3.

Row 6 As row 1.

Row 7 (K8, yfwd, ssk) twice, k6, sl 1wyif, turn, k the sl st, p25, p2tog (last st of this square and next st of Triangle 2 held on needle), turn.

Row 8 K6, (k2tog, yfwd, k1, yfwd, ssk, k5) twice, sl 1wyif, turn, k the sl st, p25, p2tog (last st of this square and next st of Triangle 2 held on needle), turn.

Row 9 As row 7.**

Rep from ** to ** twice more.

Row 26 As row 1.

Row 27 K26, sl 1wyif, turn, k the sl st, p25, p2tog (last st of this square and last st of Triangle 2 held on needle), DO NOT TURN.

Square 3

(Cable patt – worked on 27 sts throughout)

Using B and with WS of work facing, pick up 27 sts purlwise along the next edge of Triangle 2, turn. Work as given for Square 1; the p2tog at the end of the row will be worked on last st of this square and next st of Triangle 1 held on needle.

Triangle 6 worked at side edge (lace st
– decreases from 27 sts to 1 st)

Using B and with WS of work facing, pick up 27 sts purlwise along the next edge of Triangle 1, turn.

Row 1 K26, sl 1wyif, turn, k the sl st, p24, p2tog (shapes the side edge on this and every following row), turn. 26 sts.

Row 2 K25, sl 1wyif, turn, k the sl st, p23, p2tog, turn. 25 sts.

Row 3 K11, yfwd, ssk, k8, yfwd, ssk, k1, sl 1wyif, turn, k the sl st, p22, p2tog, turn. 24 sts.

Row 4 K8, k2tog, yfwd, k1, yfwd, ssk, k5, k2tog, yfwd, k1, yfwd, ssk, sl 1wyif, turn, k the sl st, p21, p2tog, turn. 23 sts.

Row 5 K9, yfwd, ssk, k8, yfwd, ssk, k1, sl 1wyif, turn, k the sl st, p20, p2tog, turn. 22 sts.

Row 6 K21, sl 1wyif, turn, k the sl st, p19, p2tog, turn. 21 sts.

Row 7 K12, yfwd, ssk, k6, sl 1wyif, turn, k the sl st, p18, p2tog, turn. 20 sts.

Row 8 K9, k2tog, yfwd, k1, yfwd, ssk, k5, sl 1wyif, turn, k the sl st, p17, p2tog, turn. 19 sts.

Row 9 K10, yfwd, ssk, k6, sl 1wyif, turn, k the sl st, p16, p2tog, turn. 18 sts.

Row 10 K17, sl 1wyif, turn, p15, p2tog, turn. 17 sts.

Row 11 K3, yfwd, ssk, k8, yfwd, ssk, k1, sl 1wyif, turn, k the sl st, p14, p2tog, turn. 16 sts.

Row 12 K3, yfwd, ssk, k5, k2tog, yfwd, k1, yfwd, ssk, sl 1wyif, turn, k the sl st, p13, p2tog, turn. 15 sts.

Row 13 K1, yfwd, ssk, k8, yfwd, ssk, k1, sl 1wyif, turn, k the sl st, p12, p2tog, turn. 14 sts.

Row 14 K13, sl 1wyif, turn, k the sl st, p11, p2tog, turn. 13 sts.

Row 15 K4, yfwd, ssk, k6, sl 1wyif, turn, k the sl st, p10, p2tog, turn. 12 sts.

Row 16 K1, k2tog, yfwd, k1, yfwd, ssk, k5, sl 1wyif, turn, k the sl st, p9, p2tog, turn. 11 sts.

Row 17 K2, yfwd, ssk, k6, sl 1wyif, turn, k the sl st, p8, p2tog, turn. 10 sts.

Row 18 K9, sl 1wyif, turn, k the sl st, p7, p2tog, turn. 9 sts.

Row 19 K5, yfwd, ssk, k1, sl 1wyif, turn, k the sl st, p6, p2tog, turn. 8 sts.

Row 20 K2, k2tog, yfwd, k1, yfwd, ssk, sl 1wyif, turn, k the sl st, p5, p2tog, turn. 7 sts.

Row 21 K3, yfwd, ssk, k1, sl 1wyif, turn, k the sl st, p4, p2tog, turn. 6 sts.

Row 22 K5, sl 1wyif, turn, k the sl st, p3, p2tog, turn. 5 sts.

Row 23 K4, sl 1wyif, turn, k the sl st, p2, p2tog, turn. 4 sts.

Row 24 K3, sl 1wyif, turn, k the sl st, p1, p2tog, turn. 3 sts.

Row 25 K2, sl 1wyif, turn, k the sl st, p2tog, turn. 2 sts.

Row 26 K1, sl 1wyif, turn, p2tog, turn. 1 st.

Cut yarn B.

Using A, work a line of four squares worked alternately in moss st and st st as follows (there are no triangles to work).

Square 4

(Moss st – worked on 27 sts throughout)

Slip the st remaining from Lace Triangle 6 on to the right-hand needle, then using A and with the RS of work facing, pick up 26 sts knitwise along edge of Triangle 6, turn.

Row 1 P26, sl 1wyif, turn, k the sl st, (k1, p1) 12 times, k1, ssk (last st of this square and next st of Square 3 held on needle to join pieces together), turn.

Row 2 P2, (k1, p1) 12 times, sl 1wyif, turn, k the sl st, (p1, k1) 12 times, p1, ssk (last st of this square and next st of Square 3 held on needle), turn.

Row 3 (P1, k1) 13 times, sl 1wyif, turn, k the sl st, (k1, p1) 12 times, k1, ssk (last st of this square and next st of Square 3 held on needle), turn.

Repeat rows 2 and 3 11 times more then row 2 again.

Row 27 (P1, k1) 13 times, sl 1wyif, turn, k the sl st, k25, ssk (last st of this square and last st of Square 3 held on needle), DO NOT TURN.

Square 5

(St st – worked on 27 sts throughout)

Using A and with RS of work facing, pick up 27 sts knitwise along other edge of Square 3, turn.

Row 1 P26, sl 1wyif, turn, k the sl st, k25, ssk (last st of this square and next st of Square 2 held on needle), turn.

Repeat this row 25 times more.

Row 27 P26, sl 1wyif, turn, k the sl st, k25, ssk (last st of this square and last st of Square 2 held on needle), DO NOT TURN.

Square 6

(Moss st – worked on 27 sts throughout)

Using A and with RS of work facing, pick up 27 sts

knitwise along other edge of Square 2, turn.
Work as given for Square 4; the ssk at the end of
the row will be worked on the last st of this square
and the next st of Square 1 held on needle.

Square 7
(St st – worked on 27 sts throughout)
Using A and with RS of work facing, pick up 27 sts
knitwise along other edge of Square 1, turn.
Work as given for Square 5; the ssk at the end of
the row will be worked on the last st of this square
and the next st of Triangle 5 held on needle. Turn at
the end of the last row and cut yarn A.

Using B, work a line of three squares worked
alternately in lace and cable with two cable
triangles at each side to keep the sides of the
throw straight as follows:

Triangle 7 worked at the side edge (cable patt
– increase from 2 sts to 27 sts)
Row 1 Using B, p2, turn, k2, turn. 2 sts worked in B.
Row 2 Pf&b (shapes the side edge on this and
every following row), p2tog (last st of this triangle
and next st of Square 7 held on needle to join
pieces together), turn, k3, turn. 3 sts.
Row 3 Pf&b, p1, p2tog (last st of this triangle and
next st of Square 7 held on needle to join pieces
together) and turn, k4 and turn. 4 sts.
Row 4 Pf&b, p2, p2tog (to join pieces together as
before on this and every following row), turn, k5,
turn. 5 sts.
Row 5 Pf&b, p3, p2tog, turn, k6, turn. 6 sts.
Row 6 Pf&b, p4, p2tog, turn, k6, p1, turn. 7 sts.
Row 7 Kf&b, p5, p2tog, turn, k6, p2, turn. 8 sts.
Row 8 Kf&b, k1, p5, p2tog, turn, k6, p3, turn. 9 sts.
Row 9 Kf&b, k2, p5, p2tog, turn, k6, p3, k1,
turn. 10 sts.
Row 10 Pf&b, k3, p5, p2tog, turn, k6, p3, k2,
turn. 11 sts.
Row 11 Pf&b, p1, k3, p5, p2tog, turn, k6, p3, k3,
turn. 12 sts.
Row 12 Pf&b, p2, k3, p5, p2tog, turn, k6, p3, k4,
turn. 13 sts.
Row 13 Pf&b, p3, k3, p5, p2tog, turn, k6, p3, k5,
turn. 14 sts.
Row 14 Pf&b, p4, k3, p5, p2tog, turn, k6, p3, k6,
turn. 15 sts.
Row 15 Pf&b, p5, k3, p5, p2tog, turn, k6, p3, C4B,
k3, turn. 16 sts.
Row 16 Pf&b, p6, k3, p5, p2tog, turn, k6, p3, k8,
turn. 17 sts.
Row 17 Pf&b, p7, k3, p5, p2tog, turn, k6, p3, k9,
turn. 18 sts.
Row 18 Pf&b, p8, k3, p5, p2tog, turn, k6, p3, C4F, k1,

C4B, p1, turn. 19 sts.
Row 19 Kf&b, p9, k3, p5, p2tog, turn, k6, p3, k9, p2,
turn. 20 sts.
Row 20 Kf&b, k1, p9, k3, p5, p2tog, turn, k6, p3, k9,
p3, turn. 21 sts.
Row 21 Kf&b, k2, p9, k3, p5, p2tog, turn, k6, p3,
C4B, k1, C4F, p3, k1, turn. 22 sts.
Row 22 Pf&b, k3, p9, k3, p5, p2tog, turn, k6, p3, k9,
p3, k2, turn. 23 sts.
Row 23 Pf&b, p1, k3, p9, k3, p5, p2tog, turn, k6, p3,
k9, p3, k3, turn. 24 sts.
Row 24 Pf&b, p2, k3, p9, k3, p5, p2tog, turn, k6, p3,
C4F, k1, C4B, p3, k4, turn. 25 sts.
Row 25 Pf&b, p3, k3, p9, k3, p5, p2tog, turn, k6, p3,
k9, p3, k5, turn. 26 sts.
Row 26 Pf&b, p4, k3, p9, k3, p5, p2tog,
DO NOT TURN. 27 sts.

Square 8
(Lace patt – worked on 27 sts throughout)
Using B and with WS of work facing, pick up 27 sts
purlwise along the other edge of Square 7, turn.
Work as given for Square 2; the p2tog at the end
of the row will be worked over last st of this square
and next st of Square 6 held on needle.

Square 9
(Cable patt – worked on 27 sts throughout)
Using B and with WS of work facing, pick up 27 sts
purlwise along the other edge of Square 6, turn.
Work as given for Square 1; the p2tog at the end
of the row will be worked over the last st of this
square and the next st of Square 5 held on needle.

Square 10
(Lace patt – worked on 27 sts throughout)
Using B and with WS of work facing, pick up 27 sts
purlwise along the other edge of Square 5, turn.
Work as given for Square 2; the p2tog at the end
of the row will be worked on the last st of this
square and the next st of Square 4 held on needle.

Triangle 8 worked at side edge (cable patt
– decreases from 27 sts to 1 st)
Using B and with WS of work facing, pick up 27 sts
purlwise along the other edge of Square 4, turn.
Row 1 K6, p3, k9, p3, k5, sl 1wyif, turn, k the sl st,
p5, k3, p9, k3, p4, p2tog (to shape side edge on
this and every following row), turn. 26 sts.
Row 2 K5, p3, k9, p3, k5, sl 1wyif, turn, k the sl st,
p5, k3, p9, k3, p3, p2tog, turn. 25 sts.
Row 3 K4, p3, k9, p3, k5, sl 1wyif, turn, k the sl st,
p5, k3, p9, k3, p2, p2tog, turn. 24 sts.
Row 4 K3, p3, C4B, k1, C4F, p3, k5, sl 1wyif, turn, k
the sl st, p5, k3, p9, k3, p1, p2tog, turn. 23 sts.

rustic entrelac

Row 5 K2, p3, k9, p3, k5, s1wyif, turn, k the sl st, p5, k3, p9, k3, p2tog, turn. 22 sts.

Row 6 K1, p3, k9, p3, k5, sl 1wyif, turn, k the sl st, p5, k3, p9, k2, p2tog, turn. 21 sts.

Row 7 P3, C4F, k1, C4B, p3, k5, sl 1wyif, turn, k the sl st, p5, k3, p9, k1, p2tog, turn. 20 sts.

Row 8 P2, k9, p3, k5, sl 1wyif, turn, k the sl st, p5, k3, p9, p2tog, turn. 19 sts.

Row 9 P1, k9, p3, k5, sl 1wyif, turn, k the sl st, p5, k3, p8, p2tog, turn. 18 sts.

Row 10 C4B, k1, C4F, p3, k5, sl 1wyif, turn, k the sl st, p5, k3, p7, p2tog, turn. 17 sts.

Row 11 K8, p3, k5, sl 1wyif, turn, k the sl st, p5, k3, p6, p2tog, turn. 16 sts.

Row 12 K7, p3, k5, sl 1wyif, turn, k the sl st, p5, k3, p5, p2tog, turn. 15 sts.

Row 13 K2, C4B, p3, k5, sl 1wyif, turn, k the sl st, p5, k3, p4, p2tog, turn. 14 sts.

Row 14 K5, p3, k5, sl 1wyif, turn, k the sl st, p5, k3, p3, p2tog, turn. 13 sts.

Row 15 K4, p3, k5, sl 1wyif, turn, k the sl st, p5, k3, p2, p2tog, turn. 12 sts.

Row 16 K3, p3, k5, sl 1wyif, turn, k the sl st, p5, k3, p1, p2tog, turn. 11 sts.

Row 17 K2, p3, k5, sl 1wyif, turn, k the sl st, p5, k3, p2tog, turn. 10 sts.

Row 18 K1, p3, k5, sl 1wyif, turn, k the sl st, p5, k2, p2tog, turn. 9 sts.

Row 19 P3, k5, sl 1wyif, turn, k the sl st, p5, k1, p2tog, turn. 8 sts.

Row 20 P2, k5, sl 1wyif, turn, k the sl st, p5, p2tog, turn. 7 sts.

Row 21 P1, k5, sl 1wyif, turn, k the sl st, p4, p2tog, turn. 6 sts.

Row 22 K5, sl 1wyif, turn, k the sl st, p3, p2tog, turn. 5 sts.

Row 23 K4, sl 1wyif, turn, k the sl st, p2, p2tog, turn. 4 sts.

Row 24 K3, sl 1wyif, turn, k the sl st, p1, p2tog, turn. 3 sts.

Row 25 K2, sl 1wyif, turn, k the sl st, p2tog, turn. 2 sts.
Row 26 K1, sl 1wyif, turn, p2tog, turn. 1 st. *****
Using A, work a line of four squares worked alternately in st st and moss st as follows (there are no triangles to work).

Square 11
(St st – worked on 27 sts throughout)
Slip the st remaining from Triangle 8 on to the right-hand needle, then using A and with the RS of work facing, pick up 26 sts knitwise along edge

of Triangle 6, turn.
Work as given for Square 5; the ssk at the end of the row will be worked on the last st of this square and the next st of Square 10 held on needle.

Square 12
(Moss st – worked on 27 sts throughout)
Using A and with RS of work facing, pick up 27 sts knitwise along other edge of Square 3, turn.
Work as given for Square 4, the ssk at the end of the row will be worked on the last st of this square and the next st of Square 9 held on needle.

Square 13
(St st – worked on 27 sts throughout)
Using A and with RS of work facing, pick up 27 sts knitwise along other edge of Square 9, turn.
Work as given for Square 5; the ssk at the end of the row will be worked on the last st of this square and the next st of Square 8 held on needle.

Square 14
(Moss st – worked on 27 sts throughout)
Using A and with RS of work facing, pick up 27 sts knitwise along other edge of Square 8, turn.
Work as given for Square 4; the ssk at the end of the row will be worked on the last st of this square and the next st of Triangle 7 held on needle. Turn at the end of the last row and cut yarn A.

Rep three lines of squares and triangles from **** to ***** (from Triangle 5 to Triangle 8) once again, working first line of Triangle 5, Squares 1, 2 and 3, and Triangle 6 into the stitches held on needle from line of Squares 14 to 11 below.

Using A, work a line of triangles worked alternately in st st and moss to make the top edge straight and to finish the throw as follows:

Triangle 9
(St st – decreases from 27 sts to 1 st)
Slip the st remaining from Triangle 8 on to the right-hand needle then using A and with the RS of work facing, pick up 26 sts knitwise along edge of Triangle 8, turn. 27 sts.
Row 1 P27, turn, k26, ssk (last st of this triangle and next st of Square 10 held on needle to join pieces together), turn. 27 sts worked in A.
Row 2 P25, p2tog (to shape top edge on this and every following row), turn, k25, ssk (last st of this

triangle and next st of Square 10 held on needle to join pieces together on this and every following row), turn. 26 sts worked in A.
Row 3 P24, p2tog, turn, k24, ssk, turn. 25 sts.
Row 4 P23, p2tog, turn, k23, ssk, turn. 24 sts.
Row 5 P22, p2tog, turn, k22, ssk, turn. 23 sts.
Row 6 P to last 2 sts, p2tog and turn, k to last st of triangle (worked in A), ssk (last st of this triangle and next st of Square 10 held on needle), turn. 22 sts.
Rep row 6 until 2 sts of triangle (worked in A) remain.
Row 27 P2tog and turn, ssk (last st of this triangle and last st of Square 10 held on needle), DO NOT TURN. 1 st.

Triangle 10
(Moss st – decreased from 27 sts to 1 st)
Slip the st remaining from Triangle 9 on to the right-hand needle, then using A and with the RS of work facing, pick up 26 sts knitwise along other edge of Square 10, turn. 27 sts.
Row 1 P27, turn, k2, (p1, k1) 12 times, ssk (last st of this triangle and next st of Square 9 held on needle to join pieces together), turn.
Row 2 P2, (k1, p1) 11 times, k1, p2tog (to shape top edge on this and every following row), turn, k2, (p1, k1) 11 times, p1, ssk (last st of this triangle and next st of Square 9 held on needle to join pieces together on this and every following row), turn. 26 sts.
Row 3 (P1, k1) 12 times, p2tog, turn, k2, (p1, k1) 11 times, ssk, turn. 25 sts.
Row 4 P2, (k1, p1) 10 times, k1, p2tog, turn, k2, (p1, k1) 10 times, p1, ssk, turn. 24 sts.
Row 5 (P1, k1) 11 times, p2tog, turn, k2, (p1, k1) 10 times, ssk, turn. 23 sts.
Row 6 P2, (k1, p1) 9 times, k1, p2tog, turn, k2, (p1, k1) 9 times, p1, ssk, turn. 22 sts.
Row 7 (P1, k1) 10 times, p2tog, turn, k2, (p1, k1) 9 times, ssk, turn. 21 sts.
Row 8 P2, (k1, p1) 8 times, k1, p2tog, turn, k2, (p1, k1) 8 times, p1, ssk, turn. 20 sts.
Row 9 (P1, k1) 9 times, p2tog, turn, k2, (p1, k1) 8 times, ssk, turn. 19 sts.
Row 10 P2, (k1, p1) 7 times, k1, p2tog, turn, k2, (p1, k1) 7 times, p1, ssk, turn. 18 sts.
Row 11 (P1, k1) 8 times, p2tog, turn, k2, (p1, k1) 7 times, ssk, turn. 17 sts.
Row 12 P2, (k1, p1) 6 times, k1, p2tog, turn, k2, (p1, k1) 6 times, p1, ssk, turn. 16 sts.

Row 13 (P1, k1) 7 times, p2tog, turn, k2, (p1, k1) 6 times, ssk, turn. 15 sts.

Row 14 P2, (k1, p1) 5 times, k1, p2tog, turn, k2, (p1, k1) 5 times, p1, ssk, turn. 14 sts.

Row 15 (P1, k1) 6 times, p2tog, turn, k2, (p1, k1) 5 times, ssk, turn. 13 sts.

Row 16 P2, (k1, p1) 4 times, k1, p2tog, turn, k2, (p1, k1) 4 times, p1, ssk, turn. 12 sts.

Row 17 (P1, k1) 5 times, p2tog, turn, k2, (p1, k1) 4 times, ssk, turn. 11 sts.

Row 18 P2, (k1, p1) 3 times, k1, p2tog, turn, k2, (p1, k1) 3 times, p1, ssk, turn. 10 sts.

Row 19 (P1, k1) 4 times, p2tog, turn, k2, (p1, k1) 3 times, ssk, turn. 9 sts.

Row 20 P2, (k1, p1) twice, k1, p2tog, turn, k2, (p1, k1) twice, p1, ssk, turn. 8 sts.

Row 21 (P1, k1) 3 times, p2tog, turn, k2, (p1, k1) twice, ssk, turn. 7 sts.

Row 22 P2, k1, p1, k1, p2tog, turn, k2, p1, k1, p1, ssk, turn. 6 sts.

Row 23 (P1, k1) twice, p2tog, turn, k2, p1, k1, ssk, turn. 5 sts.

Row 24 P2, k1, p2tog, turn, k2, p1, k3, ssk, turn. 4 sts.

Row 25 P1, k1, p2tog, turn, k2, ssk, turn. 3 sts.

Row 26 P1, p2tog, turn, k1, ssk, turn. 2 sts.

Row 27 P2tog, turn, ssk, DO NOT TURN. 1 st.

Triangle 11

(St st – decreased from 27 sts to 1 st)
Slip the remaining st from Triangle 10 on to the right-hand needle, then using A and with the RS of work facing, pick up 26 sts knitwise along other edge of Square 9, turn. 27 sts
Work as given for Triangle 9; the ssk at the end of the row will be worked over the last st of this triangle and the next st of Square 8 held on needle.

Triangle 12

(Moss st – decreased from 27 sts to 1 st)
Slip the remaining st from Triangle 11 on to the right-hand needle, then using A and with the RS of work facing, pick up 26 sts knitwise along other edge of Square 8, turn. 27 sts.
Work as given for Triangle 10; the ssk at the end of the row will be worked over the last st of this triangle and the next st of Triangle 7 held on needle.
Cut yarn and pull through last st to fasten off.

to finish...

Sew in all ends neatly. Press according to instructions on ball bands, pulling the side edges straight.

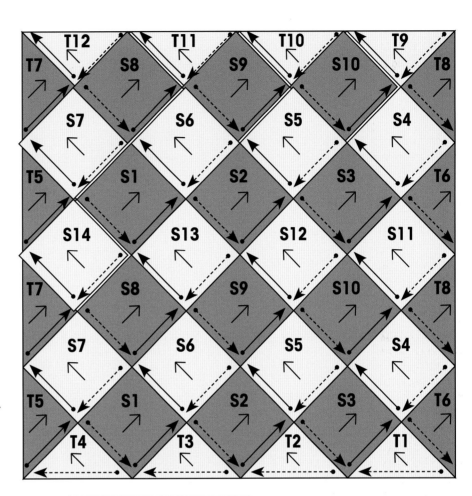

stitches to be held on needle to be worked into to join pieces together

picked-up stitches

direction of knitting

french fancies

French knitting is something that I learnt to do when I was a child, using a colourful bobbin and bright yarn to make long cords. I've used this idea to create an extraordinary floor cushion and matching chair cushion. Knitting with the French knitting cord makes huge stitches that form a bulky, heavy fabric – I used size 19 (15mm) needles to make these cushions, which should give you an idea of the weight of the cord. To emphasize the size of the stitches, I made up a multi-yarn ball to create some dynamic colour changes. The actual knitting takes no time at all, as only the front of each cushion is covered.

The technique of French knitting, whether you use a mill or a bobbin, creates a knitted-cord yarn of lovely fat stitches. The floor cushion uses a broad mix of different colour yarns to create a wonderfully variegated fabric.

YARN FOCUS

Knitting mills and bobbins work best with light-weight (DK) yarns and also smooth yarns. I chose a mix of wools and cottons for the cushions, and all went through the knitting mill easily. Inspiration for my colour palette for the floor cushion came from the garden: I used greens with soft mauves and bright yellows. I incorporated five greens ranging from light to dark: a light, zingy yellow-green in cotton/silk mix and in soft wool, a matte green in dry cotton and in wool, and a darker moss green in wool. The five mauves also range from light to dark, beginning with a delicate pink in wool, a soft mauve and a shade darker in wool/cashmere mix, then two darker shades in wool. Three bright yellows add a contrast to the palette; pale lemon in cotton, light gold in wool and a bold egg-yolk yellow in wool.

DESIGN SECRETS UNRAVELLED...

There are many ways to use this idea of making a multi-yarn ball and making knitted cord. The technique uses a lot of yarn, so rather than buying it specially, use up ends or oddments of balls, seek out discounted yarn, swap yarns and recycle pulled-back yarns. Remember to use only light-weight (DK) and smooth yarns. Choose a colour palette, making it as wide as possible to accommodate your yarn sources.

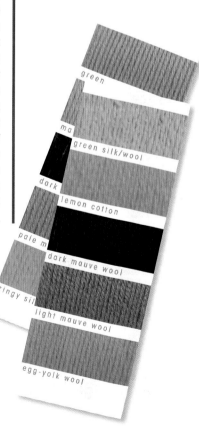

green

ma

green silk/wool

dark

lemon cotton

pale m

dark mauve wool

zingy sil

light mauve wool

egg-yolk wool

You will need to make approximately 196yd (180m) of French knitting cord to create the floor cushion. There are two ways of doing this: with a knitting mill, or with a bobbin. Both techniques are explained below.

Using a knitting mill

This is the easiest and fastest way of making French knitting cord. The knitting mill has four needles that are rotated by a handle. To use, refer to the manufacturer's instructions and use the multi-yarn ball. When you get to a knot, slow down and push the ends of the yarns into the centre. They will disappear down the centre of the cord and not show on the outside. When the cord is long enough to reach the floor, wind it up into a ball and secure it with a bulldog clip. As you knit the cord, it rotates, so winding into a ball allows the cord to untwist itself and makes it easier to knit with. Knit until you reach the end of the yarn and let the cord fall from the machine. Thread the yarn end through the stitches to stop the cord unravelling.

Using a knitting bobbin

This will take longer but is easier to carry around and quieter to use. It can be done on long journeys, anytime when you're waiting for something or someone, or when watching television. You could also get children involved with making the cord. Refer to the manufacturer's instructions and see the instructions above for how to deal with knots and how to finish. Because the cord doesn't twist during production, you can just wind it into a ball to prevent it from getting tangled.

French knitting, whether you use a mill or a bobbin, produces a thick cord of knitted stitches. Knitting with the cord results in gloriously fat and chunky stitches, as shown here.

taking the floor

MEASUREMENTS
28in (71cm) square

GATHER TOGETHER...
Materials
2 x 1¾oz (50g) balls of light-weight (DK) yarn
in wool, wool mix and cotton in each of five
shades of green, ranging from light to dark

2 x 1¾oz (50g) balls of light-weight (DK) yarn
in wool, wool mix and cotton in each of five
shades of mauve, ranging from light to dark

2 x 1¾oz (50g) balls of light-weight (DK) yarn
in wool, wool mix and cotton in each of three
shades of yellow, ranging from light to dark

French knitting mill and a large bulldog clip or
French knitting bobbin
28in (71cm) square cushion pad
2 x 30in (76cm) square pieces of strong fabric
OR readymade 28in (71cm) square floor cushion

Needles
1 pair of size 19 (15mm) needles

GAUGE
5½ sts and 5 rows to 4in (10cm) square
measured over st st (1 row k, 1 row p) using
size 19 (15mm) needles

SPECIAL INSTRUCTIONS
Casting on
Use the single cast-on for a less bulky edge. Place
slipknot on right-hand needle, leaving a short tail.
Using the cord from the ball, make a loop so the
ball end crosses in front of the cord coming from
the slipknot. Slip loop onto needle and pull cord to
tighten it. One stitch made. Repeat for each stitch.

Joining the ends
To join the ends of the French knitting invisibly,
open up one end by pulling the yarn through
the loops. Using a large tapestry needle, weave
the yarn through one open loop and then around
a stitch at the beginning of the other cord
as if grafting. Work through all four stitches
and secure the yarn end.

To make this floor cushion, you first need to make approximately 196yd (180m) of French knitting cord using a multi-yarn ball – the instructions for making this ball are given below. Once you've made your length of knitting cord, begin knitting the front of the cushion. This will show you how the colour sequences are working. You may want to change the amount of some colours that you use, or try shorter lengths to mix up the colours more. The knitting for the actual cushion is very simple: it's a basic stockinette stitch square. Only the front of the cushion is knitted; it is then stitched onto a fabric cushion cover.

Prepare your project...
The first step of this project is to make up a multi-yarn ball. You will use this ball to make your French knitting cord.

Lay out the yarns in colour groups in a row as follows: light to dark green, light to dark mauve, light to dark yellow. Beginning with the lightest green, pull out ten arm's lengths of yarn and wind it into a ball. Tie on the second yarn, leaving 1in (2.5cm) ends (these will be knitted into the centre of the French knitting cord so they will not show). Pull out eight arm's lengths and continue winding onto the ball. Knot on the third colour and pull out nine arm's lengths and wind it onto the ball. Continue in this way along the row, changing the colour and the amount of each yarn used each time (pull out seven lengths, nine lengths, six lengths, and so on). When you reach the end of the row, return to the beginning but this time use every alternate yarn. Keep working across the row of yarns, sometimes using all the yarns, sometimes every alternate green and all the mauves and yellows, or sometimes mixing the mauves and yellows. Try to vary the sequence and lengths of each yarn used. Make up one grapefruit-sized multi-yarn ball to begin with. You may need to make up more as you use it for the French knitting, as this is a process that tends to consume a lot of yarn.

Knit your floor cushion...
Front
Using size 19 (15mm) needles, cast on 40 sts.
Work in st st (1 row k, 1 row p) until front measures 28in (71cm) from beg.
Bind off loosely.

to finish...
Sew in ends neatly by pulling cord back to leave an end of 1½in (4cm). Thread yarn through stitches to stop it unravelling and use this yarn to sew the end down neatly on the wrong side. Press according to instructions on ball bands.

Making a cushion cover
With right sides together, sew the two fabric pieces together around three sides, using a seam allowance of 1in (2.5cm). Trim corners and turn cover through to right side. Turn up 1in (2.5cm) along each of the open sides and press. Insert cushion pad. Slip stitch the open edge closed.

Attaching the knitted piece
Lay the knitted piece onto the cushion, matching the edges to the seams in the cover. Pin into place. Using a strong matching thread, slip stitch the knitted piece to the cover.

MEASUREMENTS
16in (40cm) square

GATHER TOGETHER...
Materials
For main piece:
4 x 1¾oz (50g) balls of light-weight (DK) yarn
in wool and silk/cotton in each of two shades
of light yellow-green

For flowers:
1 x 1¾oz (50g) balls of light-weight (DK) yarn
in wool and wool mix in each of three shades
of mauve, ranging from light to dark

For centre of flowers:
1 x 1¾oz (50g) balls of light-weight (DK) yarn
in wool in bright yellow

French knitting mill and a large bulldog clip
or French knitting bobbin
16in (40cm) square cushion pad
2 x 18in (45cm) square pieces of strong fabric
for cushion cover
OR readymade 16in (40cm) square cushion

Needles
1 pair of size 19 (15mm) needles

GAUGE
5½ sts and 5 rows to 4in (10cm) square
measured over st st (1 row k, 1 row p) using
size 19 (15mm) needles

dark mauve

light mauve

This cushion is constructed in the same way as the Taking the Floor cushion, but is smaller. Consequently, you need to make up a smaller quantity of French knitting cord: you will need approximately 71yd (65m) of cord for the cushion, while each flower used to embellish the cover takes up about 22in (56cm) of cord. Again, only the front section is knitted; it is then sewn onto a fabric cushion cover.

Prepare your project...
Make up a multi-yarn ball as given for Taking the Floor, using half, quarter or whole ball of each of the two yarns alternately. Make into French knitting cord.

Knit your cushion...
Front
Using size 19 (15mm) needles, cast on 24 sts. Work in st st (1 row k, 1 row p) until front measures 16in (40cm) from beg. Bind off loosely.

to finish...
Sew in ends as given for Taking the Floor (page 78). Press according to instructions on ball bands.

Flowers (Make 7)
Neaten the ends of each 22in (56cm) length of cord to stop it unravelling. Twist the cord into five loops and sew them together in a circle.

Flower centre (Make 7)
Using size 6 (4mm) needles, cast on 3 sts.
Row 1 (K1, k1tbl) into each st. 6 sts.
Work 5 rows in st st, beg with a k row.
Next Row (K2tog) 3 times. 3 sts.
Next Row P3tog, cut yarn leaving a long tail and thread through rem st.
Use this thread and a tapestry needle to work running stitches around the edge of the bobble. Pull up the yarn tightly and secure.
Sew each flower onto the cushion front. Sew a bobble into centre of each flower.

YARN FOCUS
The Flower Power cushion uses just two yarns for the main piece: a smooth wool and a contrasting drier, more slubby, silk/cotton yarn. The two yarns are in a similar shade, adding a subtle tone-on-tone effect to the finished cushion.

Making a cushion cover
With right sides together, sew the two fabric pieces together around three sides, using a seam allowance of 1in (2.5cm). Trim corners, and turn cover through to right side. Turn up 1in (2.5cm) along each of the open sides and press. Insert cushion pad. Slip stitch open edge closed.

Attaching the knitted piece
Lay the knitted piece onto the cushion, matching the edges to the seams in the cover. Pin into place. Using a strong matching thread, slip stitch the knitted piece to the cover.

Each flower is made up of French knitting cord in a single strong colour, finished off with a bright pollen-yellow bobble.

denim delight

The inspiration for this throw came from my fabric stash. I had an assortment of old jeans and denim jackets, which I cut into wide strips and joined together to make two fantastic rugs. I love the way that denim alters after washing, showing wear on seams and losing colour to form patches of dark and light. I wanted to take those features and use them in a knitted throw made from denim yarns. Such yarns make a hard-wearing, heavy fabric that will get better every time you wash it, just like your favourite pair of jeans. Denim yarn is particularly good for holding textured stitches, so I used this throw to showcase such patterns.

The denim yarn shows off the deeply textured relief stitches.

DESIGN SECRETS UNRAVELLED...

You could use any yarn to work this throw and create a number of looks to complement your interiors. You could try using matte summer cottons in seaside colours to bring the holidays back home, or glossier mercerized cottons in zingy hot colours such as orange, lemon and lime for a contemporary look. Choose wool or chenille in dark, dramatic colours like greens, berries and auburns for warmth in winter. Use one colour for each panel or work in blocks.

YARN FOCUS

I used different makes of denim yarn and a range of blues from light denim to very dark navy denim. Don't worry about matching dye lots; this throw is more interesting if you mix different shades together – look in the bargain bins for end-of-range balls or for small packs in a sale. I haven't given specific instructions for changing yarns in a panel; just use them randomly to create a shaded, textural fabric.

dark navy denim

navy denim

indigo denim

mid-blue denim

light blue denim

denim delight

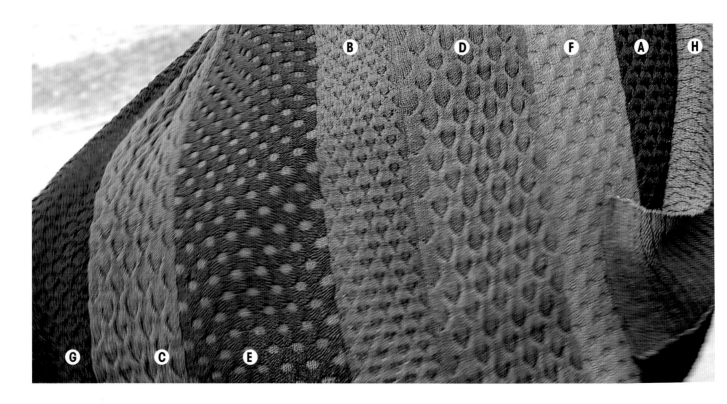

MEASUREMENTS

After washing: 56in (142cm) wide
and 52in (132cm) long

GATHER TOGETHER...
Materials

37 x 1¾oz (50g) ball of light-weight (DK)
denim cotton yarn (average 102yd/93m
per ball) in four shades of denim ranging
from light to dark
Note: use the denim yarn that is designed
to shrink and fade after washing

Needles

1 pair of size 7 (4.5mm) needles

GAUGE

19 sts and 26 rows to 4in (10cm)
measured over st st (1 row k, 1 row p) using
size 7 (4.5mm) needles

SPECIAL ABBREVIATIONS

Sl 2 [3:4:5] wyif Slip 2 [3:4:5] sts
purlwise with yarn in front of work
Sl 2 [3:4:5] wyib Slip 2 [3:4:5] sts
purlwise with yarn at back of work

The throw is made up of eight panels of varying widths that are knitted separately and sewn together at the end. You could easily alter the size of the throw by knitting more or fewer panels. The throw features four textured stitches: dimple stitch, giant dimple stitch, blind buttonhole stitch and hexagon stitch. These patterns are made by slipping stitches to make tucks and depressions in the fabric. Change the yarns randomly as you work each panel.

Knit Note: Use the different shades and makes of denim randomly for each panel. Knit some panels in one yarn, and use two or three yarns to knit other panels.

Knit your throw...
Dimple stitch panels

Gathering st: take yarn to back as though to knit, insert needle from below under 3 strands, k the next st, bring the st out under the strands

Panel A

Using size 7 (4.5mm) needles, cast on 41 sts.
Knit 1 row.
Purl 1 row.
Row 1 (RS) K.
Row 2 P1, sl 3 wyif, * p3, sl 3 wyif; rep from *
to last st, p1.

Row 3 K1, sl 3 wyib, *k3, sl 3 wyib; rep from * to last st, k1.
Row 4 As row 2.
Row 5 K.
Row 6 P.
Row 7 K.
Row 8 P2, gathering st, *p5, gathering st; rep from * to last 2 sts, p2.
Row 9 K.
Row 10 P4, *sl 3 wyif, p3; rep from * to last st, p1.
Row 11 K4, *sl 3 wyif, k3; rep from * to last st, k1.
Row 12 As row 10.
Row 13 K.
Row 14 P.
Row 15 K.
Row 16 P5, *gathering st, p5; rep from * to end.
Repeat these 16 rows until panel measures approx 63in (160cm) from beg, ending with row 8 or row 16 of pattern.
Knit 1 row.
Purl 1 row.
Bind off.

Panel B

Using size 7 (4.5mm) needles, cast on 29 sts and work as given for Panel A.

Giant dimple stitch panels

Gathering st: take yarn to back as though to knit, insert needle from below under 5 strands, k the next st, bring the st out under the strands

Panel C

Using size 7 (4.5mm) needles, cast on 37 sts.
Knit 1 row.
Purl 1 row.
Row 1 (RS) K.
Row 2 P1, sl 5 wyif, *p5, sl 5 wyif; rep from * to last st, p1.
Row 3 K1, sl 5 wyib, *k5, sl 5 wyib; rep from * to last st, k1.
Row 4 As row 2.
Row 5 As row 3.
Row 6 As row 2.
Row 7 K.
Row 8 P.
Row 9 K.
Row 10 P.
Row 11 K
Row 12 P3, gathering st, *p9, gathering st; rep from * to last 3 sts, p3.
Row 13 K.
Row 14 P6, *sl 5 wyif, p5; rep from * to last st, p1.
Row 15 K6, *sl 5 wyif, k5; rep from * to last st, k1.
Row 16 As row 14.
Row 17 As row 15.
Row 18 As row 14.
Row 19 K.
Row 20 P.
Row 21 K.
Row 22 P.
Row 23 K.
Row 24 P8, gathering st, *p9, gathering st; rep from * to last 8 sts, p8.
Repeat these 24 rows until panel measures approx 63in (160cm) from beg, ending with row 12 or row 24 of pattern.
Knit 1 row.
Purl 1 row.
Bind off.

Panel D

Using size 7 (4.5mm) needles, cast on 47 sts and work as given for Panel C.

Blind buttonhole stitch panels
Panel E

(Uses two shades of denim; dark A and light B)
Using size 7 (4.5mm) needles and A, cast on 54 sts.
Row 1 (WS) Using A, knit.
Row 2 Using A, purl.
Row 3 Using A, knit.
Row 4 Using A, purl.
Row 5 Using A, knit.
Row 6 Using B, k1, sl 4 wyib, *k4, sl 4 wyib; rep from * to last st, k1.
Row 7 Using B, P1, sl 4 wyif, *p4, sl 4 wyif; rep from * to last st, p1.
Row 8 Using B, as row 6.
Row 9 Using B, as row 7.
Row 10 Using A, as row 6.
Row 11 Using A, knit.
Row 12 Using A, purl.
Row 13 Using A, knit.
Row 14 Using A, purl.
Row 15 Using A, knit.

Row 16 Using B, k5, sl 4 wyib, *k4, sl 4 wyib; rep from * to last 5 sts, k5.
Row 17 Using B, p5, sl 4 wyif, *p4, sl 4 wyif; rep from * to last 5 sts, p5.
Row 18 Using B, as row 16.
Row 19 Using B, as row 17.
Row 20 Using A, as row 16.
Repeat these 20 rows until panel measures approx 63in (160cm) from beg, ending with row 5 or row 15 of pattern. Bind off.

Panel F
Using size 7 (4.5mm) needles, cast on 38 sts and work as given for Panel E, using one colour throughout.

Hexagon stitch panels
Panel G
Using size 7 (4.5mm) needles, cast on 32 sts.
Row 1 (RS) P.
Row 2 K.
Row 3 K3, sl 2 wyib, *k6, sl 2 wyib; rep from * to last 3 sts, k3.
Row 4 P3, sl 2 wyif, *p6, sl 2 wyif; rep from * to last 3 sts, k3.
Row 5 As row 3.
Row 6 As row 4.
Row 7 P.
Row 8 K.
Row 9 K7, sl 2 wyib, *k6, sl 2 wyib; rep from * to last 7 sts, k7.
Row 10 P7, sl 2 wyif, *p6, sl 2 wyif; rep from * to last 7 sts, p7.
Row 11 As row 9.
Row 12 As row 10.
Repeat these 12 rows until panel measures approx 63in (160cm) from beg, ending with row 6 or row 12 of pattern.
Purl 1 row.
Knit 1 row.
Bind off.

Panel H
Using size 7 (4.5mm) needles, cast on 48 sts and work as given for Panel G.

to finish...
Sew in all ends neatly. Wind off a couple of small skeins of yarn to be used for sewing up. Wash the panels and skeins (put the skeins in a small fabric bag to prevent tangling in the machine) according to instructions on ball bands. Some panels may have shrunk more than others. Find the shortest panel and pull back the other panels to match its length. Using yarn from the skein, join the panels together in a random order.

your yarn, your style!

Rework this throw in soft, pastel shades for a bedroom and trim it with a delicate floral braid, or create a warmer wool fabric taking inspiration from richly coloured, vibrant hedgerow berries.

IN THE MIX
Yarns used include light-weight (DK) cashmere/wool in soft pink and aqua, pale yellow cotton and spring green silk/cotton

IN THE MIX
Yarns used include light-weight (DK) wool in dark plum, soft raspberry and blackberry, and silk/wool in rich berry red and dark raspberry

romantic roses

Everything about this bed throw

is gloriously romantic. The colour

is a wonderful shade of dark rose in

a sumptuous and sensual silk and

wool mix that has a delicate sheen

and is smooth to the touch. The lacy

panels create a glamorous pattern

that looks like climbing roses twining

up a long stem, and this rose garden

design is enhanced by the addition of

pretty rose-petal and leaf trimmings. This

throw will transform any bedroom into

a beautiful boudoir. The pattern for the

matching Posy Pillowcase, complete with

rambling roses, is given on pages 90–91.

*The addition of the roses gives the
throw three-dimensional tactility
while harmonizing beautifully
with the main colour.*

DESIGN SECRETS UNRAVELLED...

You could work this throw in cream or
white medium-weight (aran) cotton
for a simple country cottage-style
look with pastel roses and soft green
leaves. Or you could use a warm rustic
wool to make a surprising textural
contrast with the lightness of the lace.
Work the throw in dramatic purple
with deep red roses, or an antique
shade of lilac with dusty pinks.

YARN FOCUS

I wanted a luxurious yarn for this
project and so chose a beautiful silk
and wool mix in a rich shade of dark
rose. The yarn is smooth enough to
show off the lace pattern well, and
yet has enough variation in the yarn
to add interest to the areas of plain
stockinette fabric. I worked the yarn
on a larger needle than recommended
to open up the fabric and create a
wonderful drape. The roses are worked
in fine-weight (4ply) cotton and wool
yarns in pretty shades of pink and lilac.

dark pink

lilac cotton

dusky pink cotton

dark green

lilac wool

light pink cot

dark rose silk

rose garden

MEASUREMENTS
51in (130cm) wide and 63in (160cm) long

GATHER TOGETHER...
Materials
A 19 x 1¾oz (50g) balls of medium-weight (aran)
wool/silk yarn (98yd/90m per ball) in dark rose
B 1 x 1¾oz (50g) ball of light-weight (DK) wool
yarn (110yd/100m per ball) in dark green
Roses: 1 x 1¾oz (50g) ball of fine-weight (4ply)
cotton or wool in each of light pink, dusky pink,
dark pink, lilac and light lilac

Needles
1 pair of size 11 (8mm) needles
1 pair of size 3 (3.25mm) needles
2 size 6 (4mm) double-pointed needles

GAUGE
14 sts and 19 rows to 4in (10cm) measured
over st st (1 row k, 1 row p) using
size 11 (8mm) needles and A

This throw is worked in seven panels; four feature a lace pattern of twisting stems and leaves, and these are separated by plain (stockinette) panels that echo the undulating waves. Each panel is knitted separately and the pieces sewn together at the end. The lace is created by yfwds and decreases (ssk, k2tog, and k3tog; see pages 108–109). Simple roses are added as corsages, and their stems are made from I-cord. The throw is trimmed with a lace border.

Knit your throw...
Lace Panel
(Make 4)
Using size 11 (8mm) needles and A, cast on 29 sts.
Purl 1 row.
Next Row K13, k2tog, yfwd, k14.
Next Row P.
Rep the last two rows twice more.

Commence lace patt.
Row 1 K3, yfwd, k9, k2tog, yfwd, k2tog, k13.
Row 2 and every foll WS row P to end.
Row 3 K3, yfwd, k1, yfwd, ssk, k6, k2tog, yfwd, k2tog, k13.
Row 5 (K3, yfwd) twice, ssk, k4, k2tog, yfwd, k2tog, k13.
Row 7 K3, yfwd, k5, yfwd, ssk, k2, k2tog, yfwd, k2tog, k13.
Row 9 K3, (yfwd, k1) twice, k3tog tbl, (k1, yfwd) twice, (ssk) twice, yfwd, ssk, k13.
Row 11 (K3, yfwd) twice, k3tog tbl, yfwd, k3, ssk,

yfwd, ssk, k13.
Row 13 K3, M1, k1, yfwd, ssk, k1, yfwd, k3tog tbl, yfwd, k2, ssk, yfwd, ssk, k13.
Row 15 K3, M1, k3, yfwd, ssk, k4, ssk, yfwd, ssk, k13.
Row 17 K3, M1, k5, yfwd, ssk, k2, ssk, yfwd, ssk, k13.
Row 19 K3, M1, k7, yfwd, (ssk) twice, yfwd, ssk, k13.
Row 21 K3, M1, k9, yfwd, (ssk) twice, k13.
Row 23 K14, yfwd, ssk, k13.
Row 25 As row 23.
Row 27 As row 23.
Row 29 K13, ssk, yfwd, ssk, k9, yfwd, k3.
Row 31 K13, ssk, yfwd, ssk, k6, k2tog, yfwd, k1, yfwd, k3.
Row 33 K13, ssk, yfwd, ssk, k4, k2tog, (yfwd, k3) twice.
Row 35 K13, ssk, yfwd, ssk, k2, k2tog, yfwd, k5, yfwd, k3.
Row 37 K13, k2tog, yfwd, (k2tog) twice, (yfwd, k1) twice, k3tog, (k1, yfwd) twice, k3.
Row 39 K13, k2tog, yfwd, k2tog, k3, yfwd, k3tog, (yfwd, k3) twice.
Row 41 K13, k2tog, yfwd, k2tog, k2, yfwd, k3tog, yfwd, k1, k2tog, yfwd, k1, M1, k3.
Row 43 K13, k2tog, yfwd, k2tog, k4, k2tog, yfwd, k3, M1, k3.
Row 45 K13, k2tog, yfwd, k2tog, k2, k2tog, yfwd, k5, M1, k3.
Row 47 K13, k2tog, yfwd, (k2tog) twice, yfwd, k7, M1, k3.
Row 49 K13, (k2tog) twice, yfwd, k9, M1, k3.
Row 51 K13, k2tog, yfwd, k14.
Row 53 As row 51.
Row 55 As row 51.
Row 56 P to end.
These 56 rows form the lace patt and are repeated.
Rep these 56 rows four times more.
Bind off.

Plain Panel

(Make 3)

Using size 11 (8mm) needles and A, cast on 21 sts.
Work 6 rows in st st, starting with a k row.
Row 1 K3, M1, k14, k2tog, k2. 21 sts.
Row 2 P.
Rep rows 1 and 2 10 times more.
Work 6 rows in st st, starting with a k row.
Row 29 K2, ssk, k14, M1, k3. 21 sts.
Row 30 P.
Rep rows 29 and 30 10 times more.
Work 6 rows in st st, starting with a k row.**
Rep from ** to ** four times more.
Bind off.

*The throw is edged with a pretty lace border that
is sewn into place for a final flourish.*

Lace Border

Using size 11 (8mm) needles and A, cast on 7 sts.
Row 1 and every foll WS row K2, p to end.
Row 2 K5, yfwd, k2.
Row 4 K3, k2tog, yfwd, k1, yfwd, k2.
Row 6 K2, k2tog, yfwd, k3, yfwd, k2.
Row 8 K3, k2tog, yfwd, k5, yfwd, k2.
Row 10 K1, k2tog, yfwd, k1, k3tog, k1, yfwd, k2tog, k1.
Row 12 K1, k2tog, yfwd, k3tog, yfwd, k2tog, k1.
Row 14 K1, k2tog, yfwd, k4.
Row 16 As row 14.
The 16 rows form the lace border and repeated.
Cont in patt until border is of sufficient length to fit
around throw, ending with row 16 of patt.
Bind off.

*The sculptural roses in realistic colours stand
out beautifully against the smooth and lustrous
texture of the knitted throw.*

Small Roses

(Make 15 using rose colours randomly)
Using size 3 (3.25mm) needles, cast on 80 sts.
Work 8 rows in st st, starting with a k row.
Dec Row (K2tog) 40 times. 40 sts.
Dec Row (P2tog) 20 times. 20 sts.
Dec Row (K2tog) 10 times. 10 sts.
Cut yarn leaving a long length. Using a tapestry
needle, thread yarn through sts. Pull up into
gathers. Form the rose by twisting it round and
round from the centre with RS of fabric facing
outwards. Secure with a few sts through all layers
at the base. Leave the long length of yarn for
sewing onto throw.

Large Roses

(Make 5 using rose colours randomly)
Using size 3 (3.25mm) needles, cast on 100 sts.
Work 12 rows in st st, starting with a k row.
Dec Row (K2tog) 50 times. 50 sts.
Dec Row (P2tog) 25 times. 25 sts.
Dec Row (K2tog) 12 times, k1. 13 sts.
Complete as given for Small Roses.

Leaves

(Make 8)
Using size 6 (4mm) needles and B, cast on 3 sts.
Row 1 K to end.
Row 2 and every foll WS row K1, p to last st, k1.
Row 3 (K1, yfwd) twice, k1. 5 sts.
Row 5 K2, yfwd, k1, yfwd, k2. 7 sts.
Row 7 K to end.
Row 9 Ssk, k to last 2 sts, k2tog.
Row 11 As row 9. 3 sts
Row 13 Sk2po.
Cut yarn and thread through rem st.

Stems

Using size 6 (4mm) double-pointed needles and
B, cast on 4 sts and work three pieces of I-cord
(see page 114) 24in (60cm) long and one piece
14in (36cm).

to finish...

Sew in all ends neatly. Press according to
instructions on ball bands. Sew panels together,
matching wave shapes. Sew border around edge.
Lay the roses onto the throw in three groups,
placing the stems and leaves around them (refer
to the photograph for guidance – note that one
of the three groups of roses includes two stems).
Sew them onto the throw.

posy pillowcase

MEASUREMENTS

27in (68cm) wide and 20in (51cm) long

GATHER TOGETHER...
Materials

A 6 x 1¾oz (50g) balls of medium-weight (aran)
wool/silk yarn (98yd/90m per ball) in dark rose
B 1 x 1¾oz (50g) ball of light-weight (DK)
wool yarn (110yd/100m per ball) in dark green
Roses: 1 x 1¾oz (50g) ball of fine-weight (4ply)
cotton or wool in each of light pink, dusky pink,
dark pink, lilac and light lilac

Needles

1 pair of size 11 (8mm) needles
1 pair of size 3 (3.25mm) needles
2 size 6 (4mm) double-pointed needles

GAUGE

14 sts and 19 rows to 4in (10cm) measured
over st st (1 row k, 1 row p) using size 11
(8mm) needles and A

The matching pillowcase is made from a single lace panel and simple stockinette. More roses, leaves and the I-cord stem adorn the pillow.

Knit your pillowcase...
Lace Panel
Using size 11 (8mm) needles and A, cast on 29 sts and work as given for Lace Panel of the Rose Garden throw, repeating 56 rows of patt twice and then rows 1 to 52 once more.
Bind off.

Main Piece
Using size 11 (8mm) needles and A, cast on 67 sts.
**Work 6 rows in st st, starting with a k row.
Next Row K to last 4 sts, k2tog, k2.
Next Row P.
Rep the last two rows 10 times more. 56 sts.
Work 6 rows in st st, starting with a k row.
Next Row K to last 3 sts, M1, k3.
Next Row P.
Rep the last 2 rows 10 times more.** 67 sts.
Rep from ** to ** twice more.
Work 2 rows in st st.
Bind off.

Border
Using size 11 (8mm) needles and A, cast on 7 sts and work as given for the Border of the Rose Garden throw, until border is of sufficient length to fit along edge of lace panel.

Small Roses
Make 5 as given for the Rose Garden throw, using rose colours randomly.

Large Rose
Make 1 as given for the Rose Garden throw, choosing a rose colour randomly.

Leaves
Make 2 as given for the Rose Garden throw.

Stem
Using size 6 (4mm) double-pointed needles and B, cast on 4 sts and work a piece of I-cord (see page 114) 12in (30cm) long.

to finish...
Sew in all ends neatly. Press according to instructions on ball bands. Sew lace panel onto main piece, matching wave shapes. Sew border along edge of lace panel. Lay the roses onto the pillowcase, placing the stem and leaves around them (refer to the photograph for guidance). Sew them onto the pillowcase. Fold the case in half and join the long seam. Sew the side seam.

Take care to find shades of yarn for the roses that will really complement the pillowcase. Here I chose realistic colours and used wool yarns for softness and warmth.

wobbly stripe seat

This stunning seat cushion worked in bold, brilliant colours features a shimmering pattern of broad waves that is created using the intarsia technique. You will need to follow the chart on page 95 to work the colour changes. Intarsia can seem quite daunting even for the more experienced knitter, what with all the bobbins and many colour changes. For a quick-knit alternative, I chose a very thick wool yarn that suits the broad wavy stripes perfectly. Because the yarn is so thick you can't wind it onto bobbins, but you can use it straight from the ball, winding off a smaller ball for the colours that are repeated.

A close-up of the cushion shows off the powerful effect of using such bold, strong colours; they zing off each other and create a wonderful visual statement. Made in chunky wool yarn, this seat cushion will also be warm and comfortable.

DESIGN SECRETS UNRAVELLED…

For this bold design, choose pure, clean colours that are strong enough to stand up for themselves; brights, neons or acids would be ideal for an urban apartment. Or you could go for more harmonious palettes of shades of blues or greens for a cooler look, chocolates for a sophisticated take, or startling black and white for graphic impact. The pattern could easily be adapted for a bench or window seat by simply repeating the 62 rows of the chart for the required length.

YARN FOCUS

This is such a bold modern pattern that it demanded to be worked in 'statement' colours. I chose bright, funky colours for a contemporary interior when a little extra padding is needed for a modern chair.

hot pink wool

lime green wool

purple wool

white wool

wobbly stripe seat

MEASUREMENTS
16in (40cm) square and 2in (5cm) deep

GATHER TOGETHER...
Materials
2 x 3½oz (100g) balls of super-bulky
(super-chunky) wool (87yd/80m per ball)
in each of lime green (**A**) and hot pink (**D**)
1 x 3½oz (100g) ball of super-bulky
(super-chunky) wool (87yd/80m per ball)
in each of purple (**B**) and white (**C**)

Block of seating foam 16in (40cm) square
and 2in (5cm) deep

Needles
1 pair of size 11 (8mm) needles
2 size 11 (8mm) double-pointed needles

GAUGE
12 sts and 16 rows to 4in (10cm)
measured over st st (1 row k, 1 row p)
using size 11 (8mm) needles and A

The broad waves on this versatile seat cushion are worked using the intarsia technique (see pages 112–113). The cushion is knitted in one piece, with the wavy pattern on the top, and a simple stripe pattern on the reverse.

Knit your chair seat...
Top and sides
Using size 11 (8mm) needles and A, cast on 48 sts.
Row 1 (RS) K13A, k10B, k8C, k8D, k9A.
Row 2 P9A, p8D, p8C, p10B, p13A.
Rep these 2 rows 3 times more.
Row 9 Using D, cast on 6 sts, k6D (sts just cast on), k13A, k10B, k8C, k8D, k9A.
Row 10 Using B, cast on 6 sts, p6B (sts just cast on), p9A, p8D, p8C, p10B, p13A, p6D.

Commence chart:
Reading RS (odd number) rows from right to left and WS (even number) rows from left to right, work in st st until row 62 has been completed.

Next Row Bind off 6 sts, k13A (including last st used in bind-off), k10B, k8C, k8D, k9A, k6B.
Next Row Bind off 6 sts, p9A (including last st used in bind-off), p8D, p8C, p10B, p13A.
Next Row K13A, k10B, k8C, k8D, k9A.
Next Row P9A, p8D, p8C, p10B, p13A.
Rep the last 2 rows twice more.

Commence base:
Work in st st in stripe pattern of 8 rows B, 8 rows C, 8 rows D, 8 rows A, 8 rows B, 8 rows C, 8 rows D, 8 rows A.
Bind off.

Ties
(Make 2)
Using size 11 (8mm) double pointed needles and D, cast on 3 sts and work 24in (60cm) in I-cord (see page 114). Cut yarn and thread through sts. Pull up and fasten off.

to finish...
Sew in all ends neatly. Press according to instructions on ball bands. Join the four corner seams. Sew base to sides along two edges. Insert foam block and sew remaining seam closed. Thread ties through back approx 5in (12cm) from corners.

The base of the seat is worked in chunky eight-row stripes of the four main colours.

Chart Key

A ☐
B ▨
C ☐
D ■

Refer to the instructions on page 112 ('Working from charts') for more information if you are new to working in this way.

making waves

This beautiful throw is like a work of knitted sculpture. The piece seems to shimmer and undulate, an effect created through the three-dimensional ridges that are formed by knitting tucks into the fabric. The colours of the yarn are reminiscent of wind-ruffled waves, while the yarn's fluid and lustrous texture also plays on the sea theme. This throw makes a strong style statement that is full of texture and movement. I have used the same technique of knitting tucks to create a subtly toned sculptural wall panel (see pages 100–101).

The amazing ripple effects of the throw are created by knitting contrast-colour tucks as you work.

DESIGN SECRETS UNRAVELLED...

The main yarns are medium-weight (aran) and so could easily be substituted by any yarn of the same thickness. You could choose warm wools in autumnal shades with flashes of berry colours for the tucks, or heavy cottons in hot summer shades with cool stripes of ice-cream colours. Work each panel in a different colour, use only two for graphic stripes, or shade the throw from light to dark. Because the throw is worked in panels, it is easy to change the size; knit fewer panels to make a long thin rug, or add panels for a super-sized bed or sofa throw. You can make the panels longer by repeating the pattern more times.

YARN FOCUS

This soft silk and wool mix yarn makes this throw wonderfully fluid with a watery sheen. I chose three sea-inspired shades: light grey, bright aqua and dark petrol-blue. The tucks are worked in seven shades of sea-green, aqua and grey.

light blue-grey

dark blue-green

light aqua

dark aqua

mid aqua

rippling waves

GATHER TOGETHER...
Materials

A 7 x 1¾oz (50g) balls of medium-weight (aran) silk/wool yarn (98yd/90m per ball) in dark blue
B 9 x 1¾oz (50g) balls of medium-weight (aran) silk/wool yarn (98yd/90m per ball) in aqua
C 9 x 1¾oz (50g) balls of medium-weight (aran) silk/wool yarn (98yd/90m per ball) in grey
1 x 1¾oz (50g) ball of light-weight (DK) cotton, bamboo or wool yarn (approx 136yd/125m per ball) in each of sea-green (**D**), light aqua (**E**), dark aqua (**F**), very dark blue-green (**G**), mid-aqua (**H**), dark sea-green (**I**) and light blue-grey (**J**)

Needles
1 pair of size 9 (5.5mm) needles
1 spare needle in a smaller size

GAUGE
18 sts and 26 rows to 4in (10cm) measured over st st (1 row k, 1 row p) using size 9 (5.5mm) needles and A

This throw looks complicated to make, but is in fact quite simple. The main part of the knitting is in stockinette. The throw is made up of six panels (two each of the three main colours) that are knitted separately and sewn together at the end. The wavy shapes of these panels are created by simple increases and decreases (M1, ssk and k2tog; see pages 108–109). The contrast-colour tucks are knitted together as you work each panel.

Knit your throw...
Side Panel 1
Using size 9 (5.5mm) needles and A, cast on 40 sts.
**Using A, work 10 rows in st st, starting with a k row.
Next Row K1, ssk, k to end.
Work 3 rows in st st.
Rep last 4 rows twice more. 37 sts.
Next Row K1, ssk, k to end.
P 1 row.
Next Row K1, ssk, k to end.
Rep last 2 rows twice more. 33 sts.
Work 11 rows in st st.

Tuck
Using D, work 6 rows in st st, starting with a k row.
Using A, k 1 row.
Turning Row Using A, k to end.
Using A, work 6 rows in st st, starting with a k row.

To join the tuck
With WS of work facing and using smaller needle, work from right to left picking up tops of sts of last A row before D rows, OMITTING FIRST AND LAST STS.
Joining Row Hold needles together with WS together forming folded tuck, and using A, k first st, *insert needle through next sts on both needles, wrap yarn around needle and pull a loop through both sts, rep from * to last st, k last st.
Using A, work 12 rows in st st, starting with a k row.
Next Row K2, M1, k to end.
P 1 row.
Next Row K2, M1, k to end.
Rep last 2 rows twice more. 37 sts.
Work 3 rows in st st.
Next Row K2, M1, k to end.

Rep last 4 rows twice more. 40 sts.
Work 9 rows in st st.

Tuck
Using E, work 6 rows in st st, starting with a k row.
Using A, k 1 row.
Turning Row Using A, k to end.
Using A, work 6 rows in st st, starting with a k row.
Join tuck as given above.***

Rep from ** to *** three times more OMITTING LAST TUCK ON LAST REP, working tucks in F, G, H, I and J.
Bind off.

Panel 2
Using size 9 (5.5mm) needles and B, cast on 40 sts.
**Using B, work 10 rows in st st, starting with a k row.
Next Row K1, ssk, k to last 2 sts, M1, k2.
Work 3 rows in st st.

Rep last 4 rows twice more. 40 sts
Next Row K1, ssk, k to last 2 sts, M1, k2.
P 1 row.
Next Row K1, ssk, k to last 2 sts, M1, k2.
Rep last 2 rows twice more. 40 sts
Work 11 rows in st st.

Tuck
Using D, work 6 rows in st st, starting with a k row.
Using B, k 1 row.
Turning Row Using B, k to end.
Using B, work 6 rows in st st, starting with a k row.
Pick up sts and join the tuck as given for Side Panel 1.
Using B, work 12 rows in st st, starting with a k row.
Next Row K2, M1, k to last 3 sts, k2tog, k1.
P 1 row.
Next Row K2, M1, k to last 3 sts, k2tog, k1.
Rep last 2 rows twice more. 40 sts.
Work 3 rows in st st.
Next Row K2, M1, k to last 3 sts, k2tog, k1.
Rep last 4 rows twice more. 40 sts.
Work 9 rows in st st.

Tuck
Using E, work 6 rows in st st, starting with a k row.
Using B, k 1 row.
Turning Row Using B, k to end.
Using B, work 6 rows in st st, starting with a k row.
Join tuck as given above.***

Rep from ** to *** three times more OMITTING LAST
TUCK ON LAST REP, working tucks in F, G, H, I and J.
Bind off.

Panel 3
Using C, work as given for Panel 2.

Panel 4
Using A, work as given for Panel 2.

Panel 5
Using B, work as given for Panel 2.

Side Panel 6
Using size 9 (5.5mm) needles and C, cast on 40 sts.
**Using C, work 10 rows in st st, starting with a k row.

Next Row K to last 2 sts, M1, k2.
Work 3 rows in st st.
Rep last 4 rows twice more. 43 sts.
Next Row K to last 2 sts, M1, k2.
P 1 row.
Next Row K1, ssk, k to last 2 sts, M1, k2.
Rep last 2 rows twice more. 47 sts.
Work 11 rows in st st.

Tuck
Using D, work 6 rows in st st, starting with a k row.
Using C, k 1 row.
Turning Row Using C, k to end.
Using C, work 6 rows in st st, starting with a k row.
Pick up sts and join the tuck as given for Side Panel 1.
Using C, work 12 rows in st st, starting with a k row.
Next Row K to last 3 sts, k2tog, k1.
P 1 row.
Next Row K to last 3 sts, k2tog, k1.
Rep last 2 rows twice more. 43 sts,
Work 3 rows in st st.
Next Row K to last 3 sts, k2tog, k1.
Rep last 4 rows twice more. 40 sts,
Work 9 rows in st st.

Tuck
Using E, work 6 rows in st st, starting with a k row.
Using C, k 1 row.
Turning Row Using C, k to end.
Using C, work 6 rows in st st, starting with a k row.
Join tuck as given above.***
Rep from ** to *** three times more OMITTING LAST
TUCK ON LAST REP, working tucks in F, G, H, I and J.
Bind off.

to finish...
Sew in all ends neatly. Press according to
instructions on ball bands. Sew side panel 1 to
panel 2, matching wave shapes and sewing tucks
together using free first and last sts. As you work
fold the tucks up and catch the top with a few sts
to secure. Sew panel 3 to panel 2, folding the tucks
down. Sew the other panels together, folding the
tucks up and down alternately. At the side edges
fold the tucks down and sew the tuck closed by
stitching it to the edge of the base fabric.

*This close-up shot shows the contrasting colours
and endulating edge where two of the panels are
joined. Here you can also see the effect of the
knitted tucks in toning shades of aqua and blue.*

wavy wall panel

MEASUREMENTS
12in (30.5cm) wide, 16in (40.5cm) long
and ¾in (2cm) deep

GATHER TOGETHER...
Materials

A 2 x 1¾oz (50g) balls of light-weight (DK) tweed
wool yarn (123yd/113m per ball) in light grey
B 1 x 1¾oz (50g) ball of light-weight (DK)
wool/silk yarn (109yd/100m per ball) in dark grey

Artist's canvas panel 12in (30.5cm) wide,
16in (40.5cm) long and ¾in (2cm) deep
Staple gun

Needles
1 pair of size 6 (4mm) needles
1 spare needle in a smaller size

GAUGE
22 sts and 28 rows to 4in (10cm)
measured over st st (1 row k, 1 row p) using
size 6 (4mm) needles and A

YARN FOCUS
I wanted to add an unexpected texture into
a room, especially an office or modern space full
of machines, metal and hard edges. I chose a soft,
warm tweed wool and contrasted it with a shiny
wool/silk mix. The colour is deliberately muted;
a light, almost silver, grey reflecting the materials
around it so that it fits into the colour scheme.
The tucks add a sculptural quality to the texture.

dark grey silk

light grey tweed

Like the Rippling Waves throw, this wall panel features tucks of a contrasting
colour. Unlike the throw, the panel is worked in one piece. This panel is easy
to make; just knit your fabric and use it to cover an artist's canvas. It will make
a striking piece of knitted art to grace any interior.

Knit your wall panel...
Using size 6 (4mm) needles and A, cast on 66 sts.
Using A, work 2¾in (7cm) in st st, ending with
a P row.
** Using B, work 6 rows in st st.
Using A, knit 3 rows.
Using A, work 5 rows in st st, beg with a P row.

To join the tuck
With WS of work facing and using smaller needle,
work from right to left picking up tops of sts of last
A row before B rows.
Joining Row Hold needles together with WS
together forming folded tuck, and using A, *insert
needle through next sts on both needles, wrap yarn
around needle and pull a loop through both sts,
rep from * to end.
Using A, work 2in (5cm) in st st, ending with
a P row.**

Rep from ** to ** until panel measures
17½in (44.5cm) long.
Bind off.

to finish...
Sew in all ends neatly. Press according to
instructions on ball bands. Using B, work three
wavy lines of running stitch up the panel, folding
the tucks up on the first line, down on the second
and up on the third. Stitch the tucks down on the
side edges. Place knitted fabric onto canvas panel,
making sure it is central. Stretch to cover both short
ends and staple fabric in place. Pull fabric to cover
long edges and staple in place. Fold corners neatly
and staple in place.

*The main body of the panel is worked in tweed
wool; the 'waves' are knitted in a wool/silk blend.*

DESIGN SECRETS UNRAVELLED...
I love the thought of having knitting on walls as well as on furniture as throws and cushions or on the floor
as rugs. You could knit this panel in shades and yarns to reflect your interior; work in wools for warmth,
synthetics for shine and texture, or silk for light luxury. Work each tuck in a different colour to pick out
accents in your room, or use a different colour between the tucks to make a colourful striped artwork.

it's all in
the detail...

casting on

Most knitters have their own favoured method for casting on, so I have generally not specified which method to use – with the exception of the few projects where the cable cast-on is recommended. In many of the projects I have added the instruction to cast on loosely. If you cast on too tightly, the edge will not stretch sufficiently and may break. Try using a size larger needle to make sure it is loose enough. Remember to change back to the correct size needle to begin knitting.

CABLE CAST-ON

This method of casting on is used to make a firm edge for a throw. This method needs two needles. To cast on at the beginning of a project, make a slip knot about 6in (15cm) from the end of the yarn and slip it on to a needle held in your left hand.

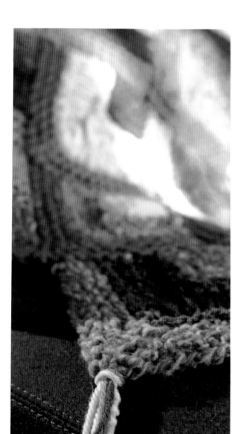

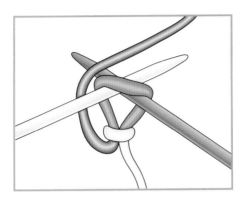

1 Insert the right-hand needle into the slip knot as though to knit it and wrap the yarn around the tip.

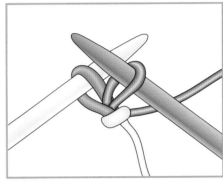

2 Pull a new loop through but do not slip the stitch off the left-hand needle.

3 Place the loop on to the left-hand needle by inserting the left-hand needle into the front of the loop from right to left.

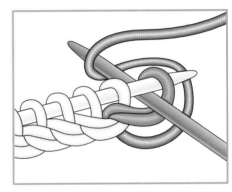

4 Insert the right-hand needle between the two stitches and wrap the yarn around the tip. When the new loop is pulled through between the stitches, place it on the left-hand needle, as shown in step 3.

Repeat step 4 until you have cast on the required number of stitches.

Extra stitches

To cast on the extra stitches needed in the middle of knitting, work step 4 only, working the first stitch between the next two stitches already on the left-hand needle.

knit stitch

The knit stitch is the classic knitting stitch, and the one that all beginners learn first. Once you know this stitch, you can start making the throws and cushions in this book.

MAKING THE KNIT STITCH

Each knit stitch is made up of four easy steps. The yarn is held at the back of the work (the side facing away from you).

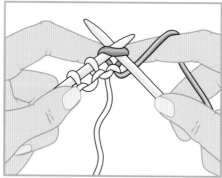

1 Hold the needle with the cast-on stitches in your left hand, and insert the right-hand needle into the front of the stitch from left to right.

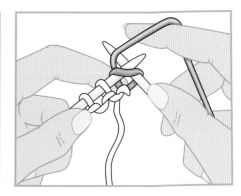

2 Pass the yarn under and around the right-hand needle.

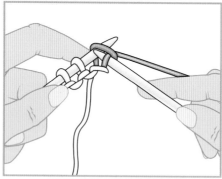

3 Pull the new loop on the right-hand needle through the stitch on the left-hand needle.

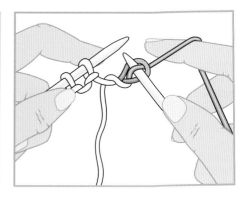

4 Slip the stitch off the left-hand needle. One knit stitch is completed.

Repeat these four steps for each stitch on the left-hand needle. All the stitches on the left-hand needle will be transferred to the right-hand needle, where the new row is formed. At the end of the row, swap the needle with the stitches into your left hand and the empty needle into your right hand to begin the next row.

GARTER STITCH

When you knit each row, the fabric you make is called garter stitch (g st). This has rows of raised ridges on the front and back of the fabric. Garter stitch lies flat, is quite a thick fabric and does not curl at the edges. Garter stitch is ideal for a project that has lots of texture, such as the On the Fringes throw – any fancier stitches would simply be lost. It's also useful for items that are reversible, as it looks the same from both sides.

purl stitch

Purl stitch is the other classic knitting stitch. Once you know both the knit and purl stitches, you can pretty much make anything. One row of knit and one row of purl makes stockinette stitch, which, with its clearly distinguishable right and wrong side, forms the fundamental knitted fabric.

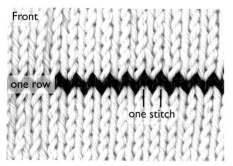

STOCKINETTE STITCH

Stockinette stitch (st st) is formed by knitting one row, purling the next row, and then repeating these two rows.

In the knitting instructions for the projects, stockinette stitch is written as follows:

Row 1 (RS) Knit.

Row 2 Purl.

Or, the instructions may be:

Work in st st (1 row k, 1 row p), beg with a k row.

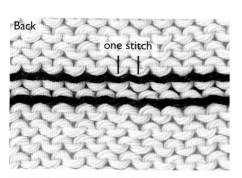

REVERSE STOCKINETTE STITCH

Reverse stockinette stitch (rev st st) is when the back of stockinette stitch fabric is used as the right side. This is commonly used as the background for cables, but can also be used as the right side of fabrics knitted in fancy yarns, such as faux fur or fashion yarns. This is because most of the textured effect of the yarn remains on the reverse side of the fabric.

MAKING THE PURL STITCH

Each purl stitch is made up of four easy steps. The yarn is held at the front of the work (the side facing you).

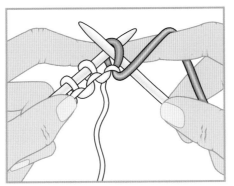

1 Hold the needle with the cast-on stitches in your left hand, and insert the right-hand needle into the front of the stitch from right to left.

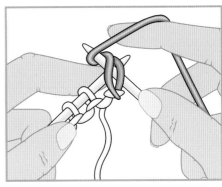

2 Pass the yarn over and around the right-hand needle.

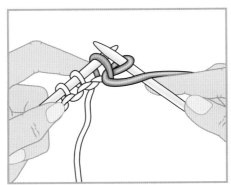

3 Pull the new loop on the right-hand needle through the stitch on the left-hand needle.

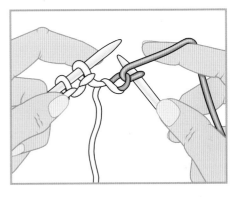

4 Slip the stitch off the left-hand needle. One stitch is completed.

Repeat these four steps for each stitch on the left-hand needle. All the stitches on the left-hand needle will be transferred to the right-hand needle, where the new purl row is formed. At the end of the row, swap the needle with the stitches into your left hand and the empty needle into your right hand to begin the next row.

binding off

Unless specifically instructed to do otherwise, you should bind off in pattern – for example, bind off knitwise on the right side of a piece knitted in stockinette stitch. The various methods are explained below. The bound-off edge should not be too tight otherwise it will pull the knitted fabric in. This is important when binding off a visible edge, as will often be the case for throws. If you do tend to bind off tightly, try using a needle a size larger than that used for the knitted fabric.

BIND OFF KNITWISE

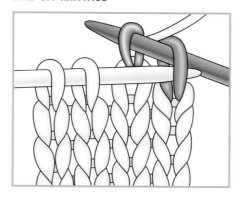

1 Knit two stitches, and insert the tip of the left-hand needle into the front of the first stitch on the right-hand needle.

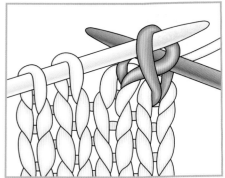

2 Lift this stitch over the second stitch and off the needle.

KNIT PERFECT

When you wish to stop knitting, but aren't ready to bind off yet, always finish the complete row. Finishing in the middle of a row will stretch the stitches and they may slide off the needle. If you need to put your knitting aside for several weeks or even months and do not have time to finish the piece beforehand, mark on the pattern or make a note of where you have got to. If you are working in a regular pattern such as stockinette stitch, when restarting again it is worth unravelling a couple of rows and reknitting them, as stitches left over time on the needles can become stretched and leave an unsightly ridge where you stopped.

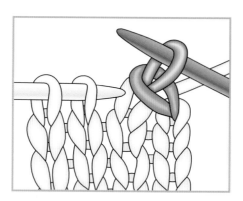

3 One stitch is left on the right-hand needle.

4 Knit the next stitch and lift the second stitch over this and off the needle. Continue in this way until one stitch remains on the right-hand needle.

Cut the yarn (leaving a length long enough to sew in), thread the end through the last stitch and slip it off the needle. Pull the yarn end to tighten the stitch.

BIND OFF PURLWISE

To bind off on a purl row, simply purl the stitches instead of knitting them.

BIND OFF IN PATTERN

To bind off in rib, you must knit the knit stitches and purl the purl stitches of the rib. If you are working a pattern of cable stitches, you bind off in pattern; once again, you should knit the knit stitches and purl the purl stitches.

beads and loops

There are many wonderful ways to add extra interest and texture to your knitting. Below we describe how to knit with beads, and how to make the wonderfully curly loop stitch.

KNITTING WITH BEADS

This simple technique is ideal for adding a large number of beads or sequins, such as on the Terrific Trimmings projects (pages 30–35). Unlike other methods of beaded knitting, you don't have to thread all the beads onto the yarn before you begin.

PB: PLACE BEAD OR SEQUIN

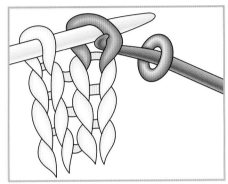

1 Insert crochet hook through hole in sequin.
2 Hook next st off the left-hand needle and through the sequin.

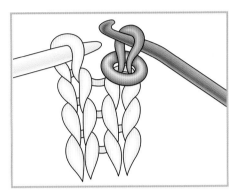

3 Place the st onto the right-hand needle without working it.

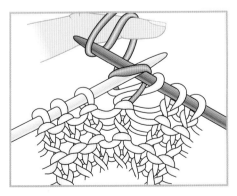

1 Knit into the back of the next stitch. Do not slip stitch off the left-hand needle.

LOOPED KNITTING

This technique is used for the frothy corners of the Life's a Beach projects (pages 62–65). The base fabric is garter stitch; a row of twisted knit stitches knitted through the back of the loop (k1 tbl) is followed by a row of loop stitches. The pattern is a two-row repeat with the loops made on the wrong-side row.

2 Insert the tip of the right-hand needle into the front of the same stitch and knit the stitch by passing the yarn anti-clockwise around the index finger of the left hand and then round the needle. Slip the stitch off the left-hand needle.

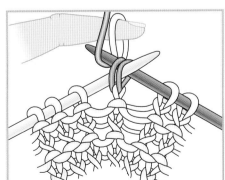

3 Insert the tip of the left-hand needle through the front of the two stitches just worked and knit them together. Pull the loop on the index finger gently to tighten the stitch. Remove finger. Repeat steps 1–3 for every stitch across the row to the last stitch, k1 tbl. These two rows form the pattern.

increasing stitches

Many of the projects in this book call for some shaping. The pattern instructions will tell you which method to use. Increases such as yfwd are used to create the holes in lace fabric.

The circular pieces of the Sizzling Stripes projects are shaped by using the kf&b increase.

Make 1 (M1)

The increased stitch is made between two existing stitches using the horizontal thread that lies between the stitches.

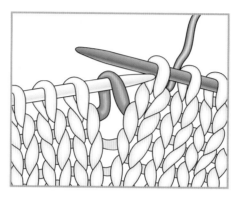

1 Knit to the point where the increase is to be made. Insert the tip of the left-hand needle under the running thread from front to back.

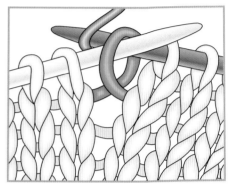

2 Knit this loop through the back to twist it. By twisting it you prevent a hole appearing where the made stitch is.

Kf&b (knit into front and back)

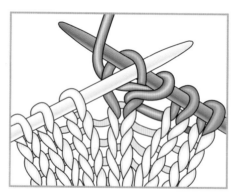

Knit into the front of the stitch as usual. Do not slip the stitch off the left-hand needle but knit into it again through the back of the loop. Then slip the original stitch off the left-hand needle.

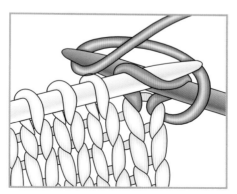

Yfwd (yarn forward) between two knit stitches

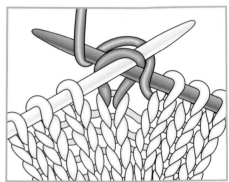

Bring the yarn forward between the two needles. Knit the next stitch, taking the yarn over the right needle.

Yon (yarn over needle) at the edge of work

Sometimes you have to work a yarn over at the edge of the work, before the first stitch. The Breaking Waves throw (pages 62–64) is shaped using this method.

Before a knit stitch: bring the yarn forward as if to purl, knit the first stitch bringing the yarn over the right needle as you do so.

Before a purl stitch: take the yarn back as if to knit, purl the first stitch bringing the yarn over the right needle as you do so.

decreasing stitches

Decreases are used to shape many of the projects and also to make a lace pattern on the Romantic Roses projects (pages 86–91).

DECREASING ONE STITCH
There are a number of ways to decrease one stitch.

K2tog

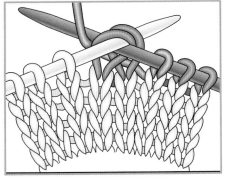

Knit to where the decrease is to be, insert the right-hand needle (as though to knit) through the next two stitches and knit them together as one stitch.

P2tog

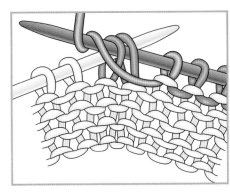

Purl to where the decrease is to be, insert the right-hand needle (as though to purl) through the next two stitches and purl them together as one stitch.

DECREASING TWO STITCHES AT ONCE
There are various ways of decreasing two stitches at once.

K3tog
Work as k2tog, but knit three stitches together instead of two.

P3tog
Work as p2tog, but purl three stitches together instead of two.

K3tog tbl
Work as ssk (or k2tog tbl), but slip three stitches instead of two and knit them together.

P3tog tbl
Work as ssp, but slip three stitches instead of two and purl them together through the backs of the loops.

SK2PO
This stands for: slip one, knit two together, pass slipped stitch over. Slip the next stitch onto the right-hand needle, knit the next two stitches together, and lift the slipped stitch over the k2tog and off the needle.

Ssk or k2tog tbl

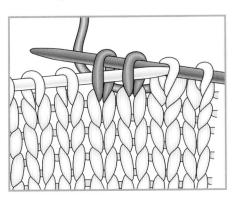

1 Slip two stitches knitwise one at a time from left-hand needle to right-hand needle (they will be twisted).
2 Insert the left-hand needle from left to right through the fronts of these two stitches and knit together as one stitch.

Ssp or p2tog tbl

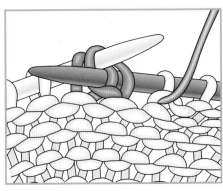

1 Slip two stitches knitwise, one at a time, from the left-hand needle to the right-hand needle (they will be twisted), pass these two stitches back to the left-hand needle in this twisted way.
2 Purl these two stitches together through the back loops.

knitting in the round

Circular knitting means that the knitted fabric is worked in rounds instead of rows; when you reach the end of a round you simply begin the next without turning the needles. You need different needles from those you usually use for knitting; a set of five double-pointed needles is used to knit circles and squares like those used for the Sizzling Stripes cushions (pages 40–43) and the Cubist Colour projects (page 56–61).

You can change onto a circular needle when the stitches become too many to keep safely on the double-pointed needles and also to knit a tube of fabric with no seams. The sides of the Citrus Squares seating cube (pages 56–59) are knitted like this. A circular needle is a length of flexible nylon wire fixed between two short needles. Such needles come in several lengths. By knitting in rounds, you produce a fabric with no seams.

DOUBLE-POINTED NEEDLES

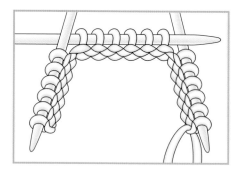 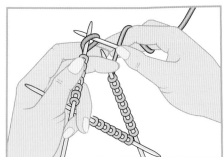

These are available in sets of five: four needles to hold the stitches and one to knit with.

Cast on the required number of stitches onto one needle and then slip them onto the other three so that each has the same number. Arrange the needles into a square, making sure the cast-on edge faces inwards and is not twisted. With the free

needle, knit the first cast-on stitch, pulling the yarn up tightly to join the last cast-on stitch with the first. Continue to knit all the stitches off the first needle. You now have a different free needle. Use this to knit the stitches off the second needle. Repeat for the remaining two needles until you reach the end of the round. Place a stitch marker one stitch in from the last stitch so it doesn't fall off the needle.

CIRCULAR NEEDLES

To use a circular needle to knit in rounds, you pick up or cast on the required number of stitches using one of the needle ends. Spread them evenly around the needle, making sure that the stitches face inwards and are not twisted. The stitches should lie closely together and not be pulled too far apart. If the stitches are stretched when the needles are joined, you will need to use a shorter needle.

To identify the beginning of the round, place a marker between the last and first cast-on stitch and slip this on every round. Bring the two needles together and knit the first stitch, pulling up the yarn to prevent a gap. Continue knitting each stitch to reach the marker. One round has been completed. Begin the next round by slipping the marker.

I have also recommended using circular needles for knitting some of the throws worked in flat knitting. Straight knitting needles wouldn't be long enough to hold the large number of stitches. All the stitches can easily be accommodated on the nylon wire and the weight of the fabric is held in front of you, on your lap, rather than at the end of long straight needles. Use the circular needle just as you would straight needles; turn at the end of every row.

cables

I've used cables on Celtic Knot Garden cushion (pages 36–39) and for one of the panels in the Rustic Entrelac throw (pages 66–73). Cables are simply a way of twisting two sets of stitches to form a rope or of carrying stitches across the fabric. Use a cable needle to hold the stitches or a double-pointed needle if you find using a cable needle too short to hold. If you find working the stitches off the cable needle awkward, replace them on to the left-hand needle to work them.

C8F (CABLE EIGHT FRONT)

Work as C4F but slip four stitches on to a cable needle instead of two and hold at front of work, and then knit four stitches.

C8B (CABLE EIGHT BACK)

Work as C4B but slip four stitches on to a cable needle instead of two and hold at back of work, and then knit four stitches.

CR5L (CROSS FIVE LEFT)

1 Slip the next four stitches from the left-hand needle on to a cable needle and hold at the front of the work.
2 Purl the next stitch on the left-hand needle, then knit the four stitches from the cable needle.

CR5R (CROSS FIVE RIGHT)

1 Slip the next stitch from the left-hand needle on to a cable needle and hold at the back of the work.
2 Knit the next four stitches on the left-hand needle, then purl the stitch from the cable needle.

CR6L (CROSS SIX LEFT)

Work as Cr5L but slip four stitches on to a cable needle and hold at the front of the work, and then purl the next two stitches. Knit the four stitches off the cable needle.

CR6R (CROSS SIX RIGHT)

Work as Cr5R, slip the next two stitches onto a cable needle at back of work, then knit the next four stitches on the left-hand needle, before purling the two stitches from the cable needle.

C4F (CABLE FOUR FRONT)

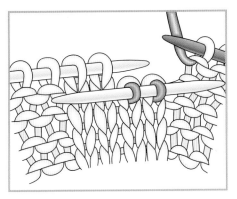

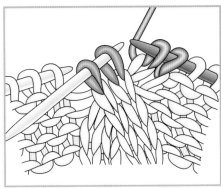

1 Slip the next two stitches from the left-hand needle on to a cable needle and hold at the front of the work.

2 Knit the next two stitches on the left-hand needle, then knit the two stitches from the cable needle.

C4B (CABLE FOUR BACK)

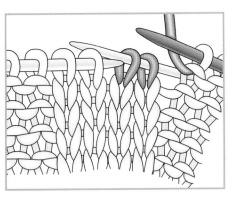

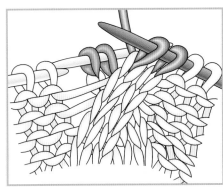

1 Slip the next two stitches from the left-hand needle on to a cable needle and hold at the back of the work.

2 Knit the next two stitches on the left-hand needle, then knit the two stitches from the cable needle.

KNIT PERFECT

Use a row counter or mark on paper each row worked to keep track of the rows between twists of the cable. To count the rows between twists of a cable, look for the row where you worked the twist; you will be able to identify this by following the path of the yarn from the last stitch of the cable to the first background stitch for a front-cross cable or from the last background stitch to the first stitch of the cable for a back-cross cable. On the row below this there will be no connecting strand of yarn between these same stitches. Count each strand for every row above the twist row.

intarsia

Intarsia is the technique of colour knitting suitable for large blocks of colour or single motifs. Unlike Fair Isle knitting, where the yarn is stranded across the back of the work from one area to another, intarsia uses a separate ball or bobbin of colour for each block. The Wobbly Stripe Seat (pages 92–95) has large areas of bright colours. In this case, the yarn is too chunky to be wound onto a bobbin, so the yarn is knitted straight from the ball. When you change from one colour to another, you need to twist the yarns together to prevent a hole appearing.

The distinctive undulating wave pattern of the Wobbly Stripe Seat is created through intarsia. Follow the chart given on page 95.

BOBBINS

In most cases of intarsia, you don't knit straight from the ball. The exceptions are if the design is very simple, with only two or three colour changes on each row, or if the yarn is thick enough to knit from the ball without becoming too tangled. With each colour change, the yarns are twisted and they will become tangled, making the knitting a chore. If you use bobbins, you can leave them hanging at the back of the work out of the way of other yarns.

You can buy plastic bobbins for intarsia, but it is easy to make your own. Leaving a long end, wind the yarn in a figure of eight around your thumb and little finger. Wind on sufficient to complete the area to be knitted. Cut the yarn and use this cut end to tie a knot around the middle of the bobbin. Use the long end to pull the yarn from the centre of the bobbin.

TWISTING YARNS TOGETHER

The yarns must be twisted to join the blocks of colour together. When you change colour, always pick up the new colour from under the old colour.

WORKING FROM CHARTS

Intarsia patterns are worked from charts. One square represents one stitch and a line of stitches represents one row. The rows are numbered: knit rows (RS rows) are odd numbers and are read from right to left; purl rows (WS rows) are even numbers and are read from left to right. Start knitting from the bottom right-hand corner of the chart at row 1.

TWISTING YARNS ON A PURL ROW

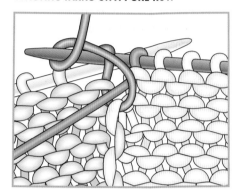

Insert the tip of the right-hand needle into the next stitch, pull the old colour to the left, pick up the new colour and bring it up behind the old colour. Purl the next stitch. The two yarns are twisted together.

TWISTING YARNS ON A KNIT ROW

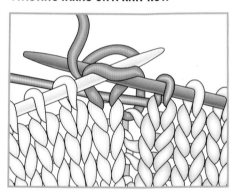

Insert the tip of the right-hand needle into the next stitch, pull the old colour to the left, pick up the new colour and bring it up behind the old colour. Knit the next stitch. The two yarns are twisted together.

WEAVING IN YARN ENDS

Weaving your ends in as you knit is a great time-saving technique. It produces a neat finish when changing colours for stripes or when using multi-yarn balls. In intarsia there will be a lot of ends where colours have begun or ended. You should weave these in as you knit or sew them in every ten rows or so. This removes them from the back where they may become tangled up with the working yarns. It also means that you won't have them to tidy up when you have finished knitting and want to get on with making up the finished project.

Weaving in ends on a knit row

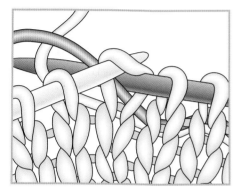 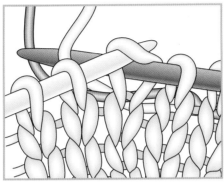

1 Insert the tip of the right-hand needle into the next stitch, bring the cut end over the needle, wrap the yarn around the needle as though to knit.

2 Pull the cut end off the needle and finish knitting the stitch. The cut end is caught into the knitted stitch.

Work the next stitch as normal, then catch the cut end in as before. If you work alternately like this the cut end will lie above and below the row of stitches.

Weaving in ends on a purl row

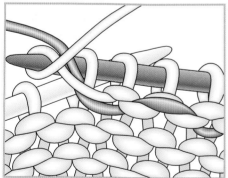

1 Insert the tip of the right-hand needle into the next stitch, bring the cut end over the needle, wrap the yarn around the needle as though to purl.

2 Pull the cut end off the needle and finish purling the stitch. The cut end is caught into the purled stitch.

Work the next stitch as normal, then catch the cut end in as before. If you work alternately like this the cut end will lie above and below the row of stitches.

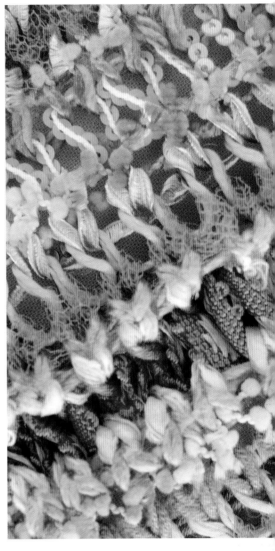

It's a good idea to weave your ends in as you work if you're knitting a project with a multi-yarn ball such as the Colour Carnival cushion (pages 48–49).

SEWING IN ENDS

Where the two colours are twisted together, you will see a line of loops. Using a large-eyed tapestry needle, darn in the end along this line in one direction and then back again for a few stitches.

embellishments

Adding embellishments is a lovely way to add a unique and personal finishing touch to your hand-knitted items. We've offered several ideas here for making your own; you could also use shop-bought trims.

POMPOM

I've used these on the Pompom Parade cushions (page 26). Cut two circles out of stiff cardboard. They should be the same diameter that you require for the finished pompom. Cut out a hole in the centre of each one half of this size. Cut a wedge shape out of the circles. Place them together and begin winding yarn around them until the hole in the centre is filled. Carefully cut through the loops all the way around, being careful not to let any yarn strands escape. Pull a length of yarn between the two pieces of cardboard, knot the two ends together and pull tightly around the centre of the pompom. Secure with a tight knot. Pull out the cardboard circles. Fluff up the pompom, trimming any uneven ends, but leave the two yarn ends for sewing onto your knitted item.

TASSELS

Wrap the yarn loosely around a piece of card the required length of the tassel. Thread a long length of yarn under the strands at the top, fold in half and tie in a tight knot, leaving two long ends. Cut the wrapped strands at the bottom and remove the cardboard. Thread one long end on to a tapestry needle, insert it through the top of the tassel and bring out 1in (2.5cm) below. Wrap the yarn several times around the tassel. Pass the needle through the middle of the wrapped strands to secure the long end, then insert the needle again up through the top of the tassel. Use the long ends to sew in place. Trim the bottom of the tassel neatly.

FRINGE

To make a standard fringe, wrap yarn loosely around a piece of cardboard the required length of the fringe. Cut the wrapped strands at the bottom and remove the cardboard. Fold several lengths in half and, using a crochet or rug hook, pull the strands through the edge of the knitted piece from front to back by catching the fold with the hook. Pass the ends through the folded loop and pull to tighten the knot. Space each bunch of strands evenly along the edge. Trim the bottom of the fringe neatly to the finished length required.

KNOTTED FRINGE

To make a knotted fringe, work as for a normal fringe, with an even number of strands in each bunch. Then take half the strands from one bunch and half the strands from the next one and tie them together. Continue this across the fringe, making sure the knots are in line. The extra knot will take up yarn so make the strands longer than the desired finished length. Try working another row of knots below, combining the original bunches again.

I-CORD

This long tube is knitted on two double-pointed needles; work on needles two sizes smaller than normally used for the yarn.

Cast on 4 stitches onto one of the double-pointed needles and knit one row with the other needle. Do not turn the work but push the stitches to the other end of the needle. Swap the right-hand needle with the left-hand needle, pull the yarn and knit the 4 sts again. Repeat this for every row. By pulling the yarn up at the end of the row, the edges of the knitting are pulled together and the tube is formed. Cast on 3 stitches for a finer cord, and 5 stitches for a thicker one.

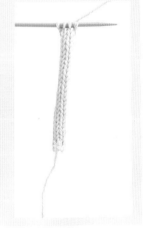

BOUGHT TRIMS

As well as making your own embellishments, you can use bought trims. Decorate cushions with braids and ribbons; look out for unusual shapes or materials. Ready-made tassels and fringing are a quick way to add movement around a throw or on the corners of a cushion. Use sequins, beads and buttons to add glitz and sparkle.

flowers and leaves

Knitted flowers and leaves are great for embellishing plain fabrics or for scattering across a throw or cushion. Work them in fine silky yarns for glamour, velvet chenille for luxury, or crisp cotton yarns that will hold their shape well. If knitted in 100% wool, the fabric can also be fulled (see page 120). Embellish the edges with beads or embroidery. We have also included a pattern for roses and leaves in the Romantic Roses projects (pages 86–91).

ROSES FOR FLORAL FANTASY CUSHION (PAGE 27)

(Make 9)
Using size 7 (4.5mm) needles and B, cast on 80 sts.
Knit 1 row.
Purl 1 row.
Next Row *K2tog; rep from * to end. 40 sts.
Purl 1 row.
Next Row *K2tog; rep from * to end. 20 sts.
Purl 1 row.
Next Row *K2tog; rep from * to end. 10 sts.
Bind off purlwise, leaving a long tail for sewing up. Curl the rose from the middle with the st st side facing outwards. Secure with a few stitches through all thicknesses on the cast off edge.

LEAVES FOR FLORAL FANTASY CUSHION (PAGE 27)

(Make 11)
Using size 7 (4.5mm) needles and C, cast on 3 sts.
Purl 1 row.
Next Row (K1, yo) twice, k1. 5 sts.
Purl 1 row.
Next Row k2, yo, k1, yo, k2. 7 sts.
Work 5 rows in st st, beg with a p row.
Next Row Ssk, k3, k2tog. 5 sts.
Purl 1 row.
Next Row Ssk, k1, k2tog. 3 sts.
Purl 1 row.
Next Row Sl2tog, k1, p2sso.
Cut yarn and thread through rem st.

ALTERNATIVE ROSE 1

With your chosen yarn and using needles two sizes smaller than those recommended on the ball band, cast on 80 sts and knit 1 row. Work 1in (2.5cm) in st st, beg with a k row.
Dec Row (K2tog) 40 times. 40 sts.
Dec Row (P2tog) 20 times. 20 sts.
Dec Row (K2tog) 10 times. 10 sts.
Cut yarn, leaving a long length. Thread yarn onto a tapestry needle and thread through sts on needle, taking them off the needle one by one. Pull up into gathers. Form the rose by twisting it round and round from the centre with right side of fabric facing outwards. Pull the rose into shape as you go, letting the fabric roll over in some places. Work a few stitches through all layers at the bottom to hold them in place.
For a smaller rose, cast on fewer stitches and work fewer straight rows before decreasing as above.

ALTERNATIVE ROSE 2
Small [Medium: Large] Petals

(Make 2 of each size)
With your chosen yarn and using needles two sizes smaller than those recommended on the ball band, cast on 3 [3: 4] sts and purl 1 row.
Next Row (Kf&b) 1 [2: 2] times, k2 [1:2]. 4 [5:6] sts.
P 1 row.
Next Row (Kf&b) twice, k2 [3:4]. 6 [7:8] sts.
Work 9 [11:13] rows in st st, starting with a p row.
Next Row (Ssk) twice, k2 [3: 4]. 4 [5:6] sts.
P 1 row.
Next Row (Ssk) 1 [2: 2] times, k2 [1:2].
P1 row.
Bind off, leaving a long end for sewing up. Sew in other end of yarn. Take a small petal, thread the long yarn end onto a large needle and use it to gather the straight edge with a running stitch. Curl the petal around itself with the st st side facing inwards and secure with a few stitches. Gather the second small petal in the same way, curl around the first petal and sew them together at the base. Continue to build up the rose with the two medium and two large petals, overlapping them.

DOUBLE FLOWER
Large Petals (Make 6)

With your chosen yarn and using needles two sizes smaller than those recommended on the ball band, cast on 3 sts and knit 1 row.
Row 1 (RS) K1, (k into front, back and front) into next st, k1. 5 sts.
Rows 2, 4, 6 Knit.
Row 3 K2, (k into front, back and front) into next st, k2. 7 sts.
Row 5 K3, (k into front, back and front) into next st, k3. 9 sts.
Row 7 K4, (k into front, back and front) into next st, k4. 11 sts.
Knit 5 rows.
Row 13 K1, ssk, k5, k2tog, k1. 9 sts.
Knit 5 rows.
Row 19 K1, ssk, k3, k2tog, k1. 7 sts.
Knit 3 rows.
Row 23 K1, ssk, k1, k2tog, k1. 5 sts.
Knit 3 rows.
Row 27 K1, sl2tog, k1, psso, k1. 3 sts.
Knit 1 row.
Row 29 Sl2tog, k1, psso. 1 st.
Cut yarn and thread through rem st.

Small Petals (Make 6)

Cast on 3 sts and knit 1 row.
Work rows 1 to 5 as given for Large Petals. 9 sts.
Knit 5 rows.
Work from row 19 to the end.

To finish...

Fold each petal in half (with RS together) at the base and sew the side edges together for ½in (1.5cm). Place the large petals side by side and run a gathering thread through each to join. Pull the thread tight and repeat through all petals again to form a circle. Pull the thread tight so the flower becomes dish-shaped. Secure the thread. Repeat for the small petals. Sew the inner ring of small petals into the outer ring.

finishing techniques

When you have finished knitting all the pieces for your project, you should press them before making up. The knitted pieces will look flatter and you can pull out any side edges so that they are straight. Before pressing, sew in all yarn ends but don't trim them. During pressing, the knitting will stretch and yarn ends can pull through. Wait until the pieces have been pressed.

STEAM PRESSING

This is the method that I use most for natural yarns such as pure wool or those with a high wool content. Some yarns with a high synthetic fibre content, such as polyester and nylon, will not stand the high temperature needed for steaming so should never be steamed. Always check the ball band before steaming or test on your gauge square first.

Using rustproof pins, pin the knitted piece out, wrong side up, onto an ironing board. Do not pin out any ribs; they will lose their elasticity. Leave these unstretched. If the piece is too big, as many of the throws will be, make a pressing board from a folded blanket covered with a sheet. Lay a clean cotton cloth over the pinned-out piece to protect it. Set the steam iron on an appropriate heat setting for the yarn. Hold the iron close to the surface of the knitting without touching it. Do not press the iron on to the knitted fabric. Let the steam penetrate the fabric. Remove the cloth and allow the fabric to dry before unpinning.

WET PRESSING

This is an alternative to steam pressing and is better for synthetics or fancy yarns. Pin out the pieces onto a pressing board, as above. Wet a clean cotton cloth and wring out the excess water until it is just damp. Place it over the pinned-out piece (avoiding any ribs) and leave to dry away from direct heat. When the cloth is completely dry, remove it. Make sure the knitted pieces are also dry before you take out the pins and remove them from the board.

SEWING UP

Whenever possible, sew the pieces together with the yarn they are knitted from. If the yarn is something that will break easily or is textured, like an eyelash yarn or bouclé, use a plain yarn in a matching colour. Do not use the long ends left after knitting the pieces to sew up with; if you do use them and you have to unpick the item for any reason, the ends may start to unravel the knitting. Use a tapestry needle and an 18in (45cm) length of yarn, so the yarn doesn't fray by being passed through the fabric too frequently.

Mattress stitch

To get an invisible seam, use mattress stitch. This is worked from the right side, making it easier to match stripes and shaping details, such as on the

top of a hat. Secure the sewing yarn by weaving it down the edge of one of the pieces, bringing it to the front on the first row between the corner and second stitches. Place the two pieces to be joined side by side on a flat surface.

Joining two pieces of stockinette stitch

Having secured the yarn, take the needle across to the opposite side and insert it into the first row between the first and second stitches from front to back. Take it under the horizontal strand of the row above and pull the yarn through. Take the needle across to the first edge, insert the needle into the first row between stitches, again from front to back, and take it under the horizontal strands of the two rows above. Pull the yarn through. Insert the needle into the opposite edge again, in the same hole that the yarn came out of, and take it under the horizontal strands of the two rows above. Continue zigzagging between the edges, working under two rows each time. Pull the yarn up every few stitches to draw the seam together – but not too tightly, as the seam should not pucker the fabric.

Joining two pieces of reverse stockinette stitch

Having secured the yarn, take the needle across to the opposite side and insert it from front to back under the horizontal strand of the row above and pull the yarn through. Take the needle across to the other edge and insert it from front to back under the top loop of the second stitch. Take the needle back to the other edge and work under the strand of the row above. Continue in this way, inserting the needle under the top loop of the second stitch on one edge and under the horizontal strand between the first and second stitches on the other edge. One side of the seam takes in one and a half stitches, and the other takes in one stitch, but this weaves the reverse stockinette stitch together so the seam is invisible.

JOIN TWO BOUND-OFF EDGES TOGETHER STITCH BY STITCH

Lay the two pieces, one above the other, with the bind-off edges together. Start on the bottom piece; weave the yarn through a few stitches to secure it. Bring the needle to the front through the centre of the first stitch of the row below the bind-off edge. Take the needle up to the top piece and insert the needle through the centre of the first stitch and bring it out in the centre of the next stitch. Take the needle back down to the bottom piece and insert it into the same hole, and bring it up in the centre of the next stitch. Take the needle back to the top piece and insert the needle into the same hole and bring it out in the centre of the next stitch. Pull the yarn up tight to hide the bound-off edges. Continue in this way, and the seam will resemble a new row of stitches.

PICKING UP STITCHES

Picking up stitches means that two pieces can be joined together without seams. Both the Hedgerow Harlequin throw (pages 50–53) and the Rustic Entrelac throw (pages 66–73) are made by picking up stitches. Also, when you add a knitted border to a throw, you could pick up the stitches for it evenly along the edge.

The Rustic Entrelac throw is created by picking up the stitches for each panel from the panel before, rather than by seaming the individual panels together.

On a bound-off edge

Hold the work in your left hand with the right side facing. With a needle and the yarn in your right hand, insert the needle into the centre of the first stitch in the row below the bound-off edge. Wrap the yarn knitwise around the needle and draw through a loop. Continue in this way, inserting the needle through the centre of each stitch.

On a vertical edge (ends of rows)

Hold the work in your left hand with the right side facing. With a needle and the yarn in your right hand, insert the needle between the first and second stitches at the beginning of the first row, wrap the yarn around knitwise and pull through a stitch. Continue up the edge, inserting the needle between the stitches on each row, taking in one stitch. If you are using a thick yarn, where one stitch may measure ½in (1cm) or more, insert the needle through the centre of the edge stitch, taking in only half a stitch to reduce bulk.

cushions

Cushions are a quick and easy way to introduce colour into an interior. Some of the cushions in this book are simply two squares sewn together, such as the Spring Greens cushions (pages 24–29). Others use circular knitting to create squares or circles, like the Brilliant Bolster (pages 40–42) or the Black and White Blocks cushion (pages 60–61). Cushions can be used on furniture or on the floor; this end use should be considered when choosing the filling.

FILLINGS

Ready-made cushion pads are available in a wide range of sizes; always buy one that is slightly bigger than your finished cover. The cover will stretch to fit instead of looking baggy over a too-small pad. Cushion pads can be filled with feathers. Many people are allergic to feathers, so synthetic materials such as polyester stuffing or hollowfibre may be a better option.

SEATING FOAM

I've used seating foam for the Celtic Knot Garden cushions (pages 36–39) and the Citrus Squares seating cube (pages 56–59). It is firmer and holds its shape better than a cover stuffed with a filling; this will move around and leave hollows in the cushion. You can buy this type of foam from fabric retailers or haberdashery stores; either you can cut it to size yourself or they will do it for you. The thinner foams are easy to cut but I would recommend having thicker ones cut by the retailer. They will be able to do it so the edges are square and cleanly cut. The foam can be bought in a range of thicknesses up to 6in (15cm), which is sufficient for floor and seat cushions. However, for the seating cube I had to have several layers glued together. Foam is also available in different densities from soft to firm; choose a firm foam to provide sufficient support. Foam can be quite expensive, so use polystyrene balls (often called bean bag filler) for a cheaper alternative. You will need to make a fabric lining to put them in; if you put them straight into the knitted fabric they will soon escape. See right for instructions on making linings.

LININGS

Cushion pads are usually made in bright white or cream fabric and this can often show through knitted fabric, spoiling the look of the cushion. I always cover the pad with a fabric lining in a colour close to that of the knitted fabric. You don't have to be very neat with the sewing as it will all be hidden under the cover, so don't worry if you're not an experienced seamstress.

Square cushions

These are simple to cover. Measure the width of the cushion pad. Cut two squares of fabric to this measurement adding seam allowances of 5⁄8in (1.5cm) onto all sides. Sew them together around three sides, either by machine or by hand. Insert the cushion pad and slip stitch the remaining side closed.

Round cushions

Measure the diameter of the cushion. Half the diameter and add a seam allowance of $^5/_8$in (1.5cm). Draw a circle onto paper or straight onto the fabric using this measurement as the radius. An easy way to do this is to tie a pencil to the end of a piece of string, measure the radius from the pencil and place a mark on the string. Hold the string down at the mark onto the fabric and draw a circle with the pencil, keeping the string taut and the pencil upright. Cut two circles and sew together, leaving a large enough gap to insert the cushion pad. Sew gap closed.

Bolster cushions

Make two end circles as described above. Measure around the bolster and its length, and add seam allowances of $^5/_8$in (1.5cm) on all sides. Cut a rectangle of fabric using these measurements. Wrap this piece around the bolster and slip stitch into place. Pin each end in place and slip stitch to the side piece.

Box cushions

These are cushions that have a depth as well as width and length, such as the Celtic Knot Garden cushion (pages 36–39) and the Citrus Squares seating cube (pages 56–59). Measure the width and length of the top of the cushion and add seam allowances of $^5/_8$in (1.5cm) on all sides. Cut two pieces from fabric using these measurements. To cover the depth of the cushion you will need a side gusset; this is created in one piece. Measure all the way around the cushion block and its depth; add seam allowances of $^5/_8$in (1.5cm) on all sides. Sew the gusset around the top piece, joining the ends at one corner. Sew the other piece to the side gusset, leaving one side open. Insert the cushion block and slip stitch closed. For the seating cube, you will have to leave two sides open to leave a large enough gap to get the foam cube inside.

Floor cushions

Because these are in contact with the floor, they need a tough fabric as a base. Use a furnishing weight fabric in a dark colour that won't show marks or stains. Make up a lining as described previously, using coloured fabric for the top and side gusset and the dark fabric as the base. Slip the knitted cover over the top and slip stitch this around the base using a strong thread and stretching the cover to fit.

fulling

Fulling or felting is the process of washing woollen fabric to produce a felt-like fabric. I have used it for the Celtic Knot Garden cushion (pages 36–39) to make the cable pattern more robust. You could also use it for throws to make them softer and more blanket-like. If you have knitted any of the throws to use as a rug, fulling will make them more hard-wearing.

KNIT PERFECT

Always test samples of multi-coloured knitting to make sure all the yarns are colourfast.

Fulling only works on 100% wool; work a sample before you knit your project to make sure your yarn will full.

You can brush the surface of the knitting when dry with a stiff brush to bring out the felted appearance; use a gently pulling or lifting action rather than a vigorous back-and-forwards motion.

Fulling only works on yarns that are 100% per cent wool or have a very high wool content; it doesn't work on synthetics, cotton or wools that have been treated to be machine-washable. During fulling, the wool expands, fibres mesh together and individual stitches close up to form a soft fabric with a brushed appearance. The finished fabric will also shrink by up to 10% in length and width, although this varies with yarn and length of fulling. You should always knit the item bigger than you want it. Always do a test sample before fulling your knitted item; measure the sample so you can see how much it shrinks.

HAND FULLING

This is ideal for smaller items like cushions or pieces where you want to have more control over the finished size. Fulling depends on extremes of temperature, going from hot to cold, agitation by kneading and the use of soap; I use an olive oil soap. Do not use detergent or washing powder. Immerse the sample in hot (not boiling) water, using gloves to protect your hands. Rub the sample with the soap and start kneading the fabric without pulling, stretching or rubbing the knitting together. Remove the sample from the water frequently to check the fulling process. Rinse the soap out in cold water and pull the sample gently. If the stitches still move apart easily, continue the fulling. Keep up the temperature of the hot water. Stop when the fabric is dense and has a fuzzy appearance. Rinse the soap out and squeeze (do not wring) to remove excess water. Roll the sample up in a towel to soak up any remaining moisture and then lay it out flat, away from direct heat, to dry. Measure it and compare with the previous measurements; this will give you a guide to how much your knitted item will shrink.

BY MACHINE

Use laundry soap suitable for a machine (not detergent). Set the machine on small load, soiled rather than delicate cycle and the shortest hot wash/cold rinse cycle. Put the knitted piece into the machine and run it through the cycle. Do not let it spin dry. If you have a top-loader machine, open it from time to time to check progress. At the end of the cycle, if the piece hasn't fulled correctly, put it through again. Adding pairs of old jeans (colourfast) can help the fulling process because the knitted fabric has something to rub against for extra abrasion. Repeat until you have achieved the effect you want.

Felting the Celtic Knot Garden floor cushion enhances the cable pattern on the front of the cushion and makes it stand out more clearly against the background of reverse stockinette stitch.

troubleshooting

Even the most accomplished knitters make mistakes and come up against challenges, so don't be disheartened if you go wrong occasionally. These techniques show you the easy way to rectify your mistakes and find the way forward.

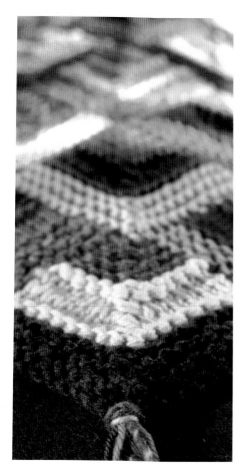

DROPPED STITCHES

A dropped stitch is a stitch that has fallen off your needle and has unravelled down a few rows, creating a ladder. The sooner you spot that you have dropped a stitch, the easier it is to rectify the mistake. Get into the habit of checking your knitting every few rows.

Knit stitch dropped one row below

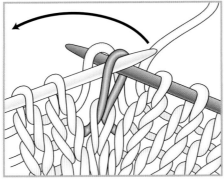

Insert the right needle through the front of the dropped stitch and then pick up the strand of yarn behind it. With the tip of the left needle, pass the stitch over the strand and off the needle.

Purl stitch dropped one row below

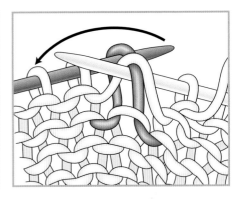

Insert the right needle through the back of the dropped stitch and then pick up the yarn strand in front of it. With the left needle, pass the stitch over the strand and off the needle.

Stitch dropped several rows below

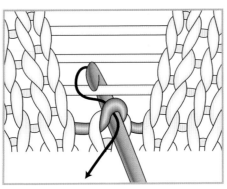

Find the dropped stitch – it will be a loop at the base of a ladder of strands of yarn. Insert a crochet hook through the front of the loop of the dropped stitch, catch the yarn strand immediately above it and pull through the stitch. Repeat for all the strands of the ladder until you reach the top. Slip the stitch back onto the left-hand needle.

To pick up a dropped purl stitch, work as given for a knit stitch but turn your work around so that you are working on the wrong side of the fabric. If more than one stitch has been dropped, slip the others on to a safety pin to stop them running any further, while you pick them up one by one. If you drop a stitch and do not notice it until a lot of knitting later, the ladder will have closed up at the top and there will be no strands of yarn to pick up with the crochet hook. Unfortunately, the only solution is to unravel your work back to the dropped stitch. If you try to pick it up by stealing yarn from the neighbouring stitches, it will create an area of tightened stitches and spoil your knitting.

UNRAVELLING ONE ROW

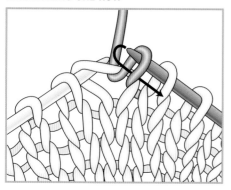

If you have made an error in the stitches that you have just worked on the right needle, for example in a stitch pattern or knitting when you should have purled, there is no need to take the work off the needle to unravel back to that point. You can just unravel, stitch by stitch, back to the error. Insert the left needle into the stitch below from the front, drop the stitch off the right needle and pull the yarn. Repeat this for each stitch back to the error. Work in the same way for purl stitches.

UNRAVELLING SEVERAL ROWS

If you have to unravel several rows, slip the needles out of the stitches carefully, gather the work up into one hand and unravel each row to the row above the error. Do not be tempted to lay the work out flat to do this, as you are more likely to pull the stitches roughly, which often results in you pulling out more than you want. Replace the stitches on to the needle and then unravel the last row carefully as given above. By doing this you have more control over the final row and are less likely to drop or miss any stitches. If you find that after unravelling, your needle is facing the wrong way, slip the stitches purlwise back onto another needle so that you are ready to knit. If you have a suitably sized double-pointed or circular needle, you can use this and then be able to work straight off either end of it.

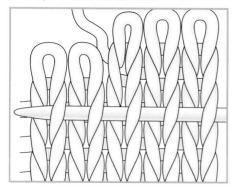

If you are using a slippery yarn or one that will not unravel easily, such as a hairy yarn, or if you are nervous about dropping stitches during unravelling, you can pick up stitches in the row below the error and then unravel knowing the stitches are safe on a needle. Take a spare needle that is smaller than that used for the knitting and weave it through the first loop and over the second loop of each stitch on the row below the mistake. Then pull the work back to these stitches. Make sure you put aside the smaller needle and pick up the correct size to continue knitting.

If you are working a cable or stitch pattern, you should pick the nearest row to the error without too much patterning and where you can see the stitches clearly.

RUNNING OUT OF YARN

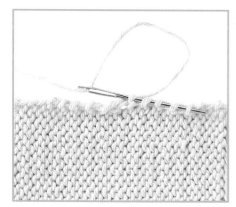

When you run out of yarn and need to start a new ball or need to change to another colour, always start it at the beginning of a row or at a seam edge where the ends can be woven in neatly.

Simply drop the old yarn, wrap the new yarn around the needle and work a few stitches. Tie the two ends securely together at the beginning of the row so neither one will work its way free and unravel your stitches. When you have finished the piece, undo the knot and weave one end up the edge for a couple of inches, and then double back

SPLIT YARN

You can easily split a strand of yarn if you are working fast, or, if you are using a yarn mix of several strands, it is easy to miss working through one of the strands. You should go back and rework it correctly, since any split like this will show up on your fabric. Use one of the unravelling methods described to go back to the split stitch.

INCOMPLETE STITCHES

These occur where you have wrapped the yarn around the needle but it has not been pulled through the old stitch to form a new stitch. The yarn strand will be on the needle next to the unworked stitch. Work the stitch properly with the yarn strand as given for dropped stitches.

CABLES

If you have twisted a cable the wrong way, and you have spotted it within a few rows, unravel the cable stitches only and reknit by using the long loops of yarn released by unravelling. If the error is a long way down the piece and the cable has been twisted again after the error, you will have to unravel the work and reknit all of it.

SNAGGED STITCHES

If you snag a stitch, a loop of yarn is pulled out, drawing up tightly several stitches around it. Using a tapestry needle, ease the extra yarn back through the distorted stitches, one by one, starting with the stitch closest to the snag and yarn loop.

over a few stitches to secure the end. Make sure you haven't pulled it too tightly and distorted the edge. Weave the other end down the edge using the same method.

If you are coming to the end of a ball, to see if you have enough yarn to work one more row, lay the knitting flat and measure the yarn four times across the width. This will be sufficient to work one row of stockinette stitch; textured and cabled fabric will need more yarn. When in doubt, join in a new ball of yarn to avoid running out of yarn halfway through and having to unravel stitches.

aftercare

Hand-knitted items need to be looked after with some care and love. After you have taken all the effort to make something beautiful, spend time keeping it looking good.

KNIT PERFECT

If in doubt about how your knitted throw or cushion will wash, try washing your gauge swatch gently and see how that reacts. If nothing serious happens, then you should be able to hand-wash your knitting carefully.

Hand-dyed yarns, dark colours and some denim yarns contain a lot of excess dye that will wash out. Wash these yarns separately.

KNITTING NOTEBOOK

I always keep a ball band from each piece of knitting that I do pasted into a notebook. I also keep a small wrapping of the yarn, as a reminder and also for any mending that I might have to do in the future. The care instructions on the ball band are the best advice to follow when cleaning your knitted items. Instead of writing out long instructions, yarn companies use the same care symbols that are found on garments. Look out for yarns that should be dry cleaned only.

LARGE ITEMS

It isn't necessary to wash throws and cushions as often as you would knitted garments; large throws are very heavy when wet and take a long time to dry. A weekly shake outside to remove dust will be sufficient for a throw draped over furniture, or use the furniture nozzle on a vacuum cleaner to give it a deeper clean. If you do get a stain on it, treat the stain individually and as quickly as possible using a spot stain remover; read the manufacturer's instructions carefully before applying. Throws used as blankets will need washing more often; this is best done in the washing machine following the instructions below.

WASHING

This is suitable for cushion covers and smaller throws or those knitted in fragile yarns such as silk. Read the care instructions on the ball band; the yarn may be dry-clean only. Before washing, remove any non-washable trims. Usually any trim that you buy will have care instructions with it. The washing information below refers to both natural and synthetic fibres (that are suitable for hand-washing).

Use cool or lukewarm water and use the same temperature for washing and rinsing, avoiding extremes of temperature. Using a sink or large washing-up bowl, dissolve soap flakes or a special wool-washing solution in lukewarm water. If the soap flakes don't dissolve, add them to hot water, dissolve them and then add plenty of cold water for the right temperature. Lay the knitted item flat and squeeze the soap through the fibres; do not rub or twist the knitting. Take it out of the water, supporting its weight with both hands to stop it stretching. Squeeze out the excess soap and water; do not wring, you will distort the stitches.

RINSING

Refill the sink with clear water of the same temperature as that used for washing. Again, squeeze the water through the knitting; do not pull it out of the water as it is very heavy when waterlogged and will stretch. Rinse it several times, replacing the water each time, until the water runs clear of soap. Take it out of the water, supporting its weight and squeeze out the excess water.

DRYING

Roll the knitting in a colourfast towel to soak up the water. Lay it out flat on a dry towel, pull it back into shape and straighten edges, and leave to dry away from direct heat. If it has any creases or is out of shape when dry, steam press it (see page 116). If it is a large item, such as a throw, or you are washing several items, you can use the spin cycle on your washing machine to remove excess water. Place the knitting in a pillowcase or duvet cover and tie the end closed. This will stop the knitting being stretched and the stitches catching on anything. Lay the knitting out flat to dry completely. Never use a tumble dryer or hang large heavy pieces on the washing line as they will stretch.

MACHINE WASHING

You should use a delicates or cool wash cycle with a short spin. Place the knitting in a pillowcase or duvet cover, tying the end closed. Remove the knitting as soon as the wash has ended, otherwise it will be badly creased. Lay out flat to dry.

STORING KNITTING

Store knitting neatly folded in clean, fabric bags to protect them from dust. Fabric bags will allow the knitting to breathe; plastic bags tend to make natural fibres sweat and become damp. Add a moth-repellent, such as moth balls, to wool items. Air the knitting outside before use.

yarns used

Below are listed the specific yarns that were used for the projects in this book, should you wish to recreate them exactly as we have. Yarn companies frequently discontinue colours or yarns, and replace them with new yarns. Therefore, you may find that some of the yarns or colours below are no longer available. However, by referring to the yarn descriptions on the project pages, you should have no trouble finding a substitute.

SUBSTITUTING YARNS

To work out how much replacement yarn you need, just follow these simple steps. Use it for each colour or yarn used in the project.

1 The number of balls of the recommended yarn x the number of yards/metres per ball = A

2 The number of yards/metres per ball of the replacement yarn = B

3 A ÷ B = number of balls of replacement yarn.

Page 20 On the Fringes
Some of the yarns used:
Sirdar Boa
Debbie Bliss Soho
Rowan Cotton Glace
GGH Domino and Velour
Patons Essence

Page 24 Spring Greens
Shake Your Tail Feather
5 x 1¾oz (50g) balls of Louisa Harding Kashmir Aran (55% merino/35% microfibre/10% cashmere – 83yd/75m per ball) in shade 06

Sequins and Spangles
5 x 1¾oz (50g) balls of Rowan Classic Natural Silk Aran (73% viscose/15% silk/12% linen – 71yd/65m per ball) in shade 462

Pompom Parade
A 5 x 1¾oz (50g) balls of Rare Yarns Cocoon (70% merino/15% alpaca/7.5% silk/7.5% mohair – 110yd/100m per ball) in Jade
1 x 1¾oz (50g) ball of Rare Yarns Misty (50% alpaca/30% mohair/20% merino – 110yd/100m per ball) in Jade
1x 1¾oz (50g) ball of Rare Yarns Astrakhan (80% alpaca/20% mohair – 85yd/77m per ball) in Jade
1 x 1¾oz (50g) ball of Rare Yarns Slub (30% suri alpaca/40% tencel/20% acrylic/10% merino – 73yd/67m per ball) in Fern

Floral Fantasy
A 4 x 1¾oz (50g) balls of Kaalund Silk-stralis (50% silk/50% wool – 131yd/120m per ball) in Kikuyu
B 3 x 11yd (10m) skeins of Kaalund Silk Strands (100% silk) in each of Fuchsia, Nectarine and Magnolia
C 2 x 11yd (10m) skeins of Kaalund Silk Strands (100% silk) in Moss

Page 30 Terrific Trimmings
Sequinned Shimmer
A 10 x 1¾oz (50g) balls of Lang Yarns Silkdream (50% merino/50% silk – 98yd/90m per ball) in shade 80
1 x ⅞oz (25g) ball of Rowan Lurex Shimmer (80% viscose/20% metallized polyester – 104yd/95m per ball) in each of shades 332 (**B**) and 338 (**C**)

Bead Me Up!
3 x 1¾oz (50g) balls of Crystal Palace Yarns Party (100% nylon – 87yd/80m per ball) in shade 203

Page 36 Celtic Knot Garden
14 x 1¾oz (50g) balls of Rowan Country (100% wool – 55yd/50m per ball) in shade 651

Page 40 Sizzling Stripes
Brilliant Bolster
A 1 x 1¾oz (50g) ball of Patons Zhivago (50% tencel/50% acrylic – 93yd/85m per ball) in shade 4433
1 x 1¾oz (50g) ball of Jaeger Matchmaker DK (100% merino wool – 131yd/120m per ball) in each of shades 655, 656 and 876
1 x 1¾oz (50g) ball of Jaeger Extra Fine Merino Aran (100% merino wool – 95yd/87m per ball) in shade 552

1 x 1¾oz (50g) ball of Debbie Bliss Baby Cashmerino (55% merino wool/33% microfibre/12% cashmere – 136yd/125m per ball) in shade 700
1 x 1¾oz (50g) ball of Debbie Bliss Cashmerino Aran (55% merino wool/33% microfibre/12% cashmere – 98yd/90m per ball) in shade 610

B 1 x 1¾oz (50g) ball of Patons Diploma Gold DK (55% wool/25% acrylic/20% nylon – 131yd/120m per ball) in shade 6151
1 x 1¾oz (50g) ball of Patons Fairytale Colour 4 Me DK (100% wool – 98yd/90m per ball) in shade 4967
1 x 1¾oz (50g) ball of Patons 100% cotton DK (100% cotton – 230yd/210m per ball) in shade 2724
1 x ⅞oz (25g) ball of Madeira Nora (80% viscose/20% metallized polyester – 110yd/100m per ball) in shade 315

Purple Patch
A 2 x 1¾oz (50g) ball of Jaeger Matchmaker DK (100% merino wool – 131yd/120m per ball) in shade 897 Azalea
B 1 x 1¾oz (50g) ball of Rowan Calmer (75% cotton/25% acrylic – 175yd/160m per ball) in shade 478 Joy
C 2 x ⅞oz (25g) ball of Twilley's Goldfingering (80% viscose/20% metallized polyester – 110yd/100m per ball) in WG60 Purple

Page 44 Mixing it Up
Mixed Messages
A 1 x 1¾oz (50g) ball of Rowan Summer Tweed (70% silk/30% cotton – 118yd/108m per ball) in shade 508 Cream
B 1 x 1¾oz (50g) ball of Rowan Cotton Braid (68% cotton/22% viscose/10% linen – 55yd/50m per ball) in shade 358 Cream
C 1 x 1¾oz (50g) ball of Rowan Denim (100% cotton – 102yd/93m per ball) in shade 324 Cream
D 1 x 1¾oz (50g) ball of GGH Velour (100% nylon – 64yd/58m per ball) in shade 01 Cream
E 1 x 1¾oz (50g) ball of GGH Domino (44% cotton/43% acrylic/13% polyester – 137yd/125m per ball) in shade 01 Cream
F 1 x 3½oz (100g) ball of Patons Mercerised Cotton DK (100% cotton – 230yd/210m per ball) in shade 2692 Cream
C 1 x ball of undyed cotton parcel string

Colour Carnival

A 1 x 1¾oz (50g) ball of Debbie Bliss Cathay (50% cotton/35% viscose microfibre/15% silk – 109yd/100m per ball) in shade 12024 Pink

B 1 x 1¾oz (50g) ball of Louisa Harding Flotsam (40% cotton/35% polyamide/10% acrylic/10% viscose/5% acetate – 79yd/72m per ball) in shade 10

C 1 x ⅞oz (25g) ball of Louisa Harding Coquette (85% polyester/15% paillettes – 73yd/67m per ball) in shade 03

D 1 x 1¾oz (50g) ball of Trendsetter Yarns Pinot (100% polyamide – 90yd/85m per ball) in shade 1030

E 1 x 1¾oz (50g) ball of Crystal palace Yarns Party (100% nylon – 87yd/79m per ball) in shade 203 Celery Green

F 1 x 3½oz (100g) ball of Art Yarns Regal Silk (100% silk – 163yd/149m per ball) in shade 107

G 1m of pink nylon net cut into ½in (1.5cm) wide strips

Page 50 Patchwork Pieces
Hedgerow Harlequin

1 x 3½oz (100g) hank of Colinette Prism (50% wool/50% cotton – 131yd/120m per hank) in shade 113

2 x 1¾oz (50g) hanks of Crystal Palace Yarns Cotton Chenille (100% cotton – 98yd/90m per hank) in shade 2615

1 x 3½oz (100g) hank of Debbie Bliss Donegal Chunky Tweed (100% wool – 110yd/100m per hank) in shade 11

2 x 1¾oz (50g) balls of Debbie Bliss Cashmerino Aran (55% merino/33% microfibre/12% cashmere – 98yd/90m per ball) in shade 502

2 x 1¾oz (50g) balls of Debbie Bliss Merino Aran (100% merino – 85yd/78m per ball) in shade 006

2 x 1¾oz (50g) balls of Debbie Bliss Cashmerino Chunky (55% merino/33% microfibre/12% cashmere – 71yd/65m per ball) in shade 008

2 x 1¾oz (50g) balls of Jaeger Matchmaker Merino DK (100% merino – 131yd/120m per ball) in each of shades 877, 898 and 746

2 x 1¾oz (50g) balls of Lang Yarns York (30% wool/40% nylon/30% acrylic – 76yd/70m per ball) in each of shades 16 and 46

2 x 1¾oz (50g) hanks of Noro Blossom (40% wool/30% kid mohair/20% silk/10% nylon – 95yd/87m per hank) in shade 19

2 x 3½oz (100g) hanks of Noro Iro (75% wool/25% silk – 131yd/120m per hank) in shade 9

2 x 1¾oz (50g) balls of Rare Yarns Essentials Cocoon (70% merino/15% alpaca/7.5% silk /7.5% mohair – 110yd/100m per ball) in shade Persimmon

1 x 1¾oz (50g) balls of Rowan Felted Tweed (50% merino/25% alpaca/25% viscose – 191yd/175m per ball) in shade 154

2 x 1¾oz (50g) hanks of Rowan Summer Tweed (70% silk/30% cotton – 118yd/108m per hank) in shade 522

2 x 1¾oz (50g) balls of Rowan Scottish Tweed DK (100% wool – 123yd/113m per ball) in shade 017

2 x 1¾oz (50g) balls of Rowan Wool Cotton (50% merino/50% cotton – 123yd/113m per ball) in shade 910

Springtime Shades

1 x 1¾oz (50g) ball of each of:

Debbie Bliss Baby Cashmerino (55% merino/33% microfibre/12% cashmere – 136yd/125m per ball) in shade 2

Debbie Bliss Pure Cotton (100% cotton – 90yd/82m per ball) in shade 12

Debbie Bliss Donegal Luxury Tweed (85% wool/15% angora) in shade 12

Rowan Damask (57% viscose/22% linen/21% acrylic – 115yd/105m per ball) in shade 45

Rowan Bamboo Tape (100% bamboo – 82yd/75m per ball) in shade 704

Rowan Classic Yarns Cashcotton DK (35% cotton/25% polyamide/18% angora/13% viscose/9% cashmere – 142yd/130m per ball) in shade 603

Rowan Classic Yarns Bamboo Soft (100% bamboo – 112yd/102m per ball) in shade 105

Rowan Classic Yarns Luxury Cotton DK (50% cotton/45% viscose/5% silk – 104yd/95m per ball) in shade 260

Sirdar Baby Bamboo (80% bamboo/20% wool – 104yd/95m per ball) in shade 133

Page 56 Cubist Colours
Citrus Squares

1 x 1¾oz (50g) ball of Debbie Bliss Cotton DK (100% cotton – 92yd/84m per ball) in shade 35 plus 2 x ⅞oz (25g) balls of Madeira Nora (80% viscose/20% metallized polyester – 110yd/100m per ball) in shade 321 (**A**)

2 x 1¾oz (50g) balls of Rowan Handknit DK (100% cotton – 93yd/85m per ball) in each of shades 319 (**B**), 320 (**G**) and 325 (**H**)

2 x 1¾oz (50g) balls of Rowan Wool Cotton (50% merino/50% cotton – 123yd/113m per ball) in shade 901 (**C**)

2 x 1¾oz (50g) balls of Rowan 4ply Cotton (100% cotton – 186yd/170m per ball) in shade 133 (**D**)

2 x 1¾oz (50g) balls of Debbie Bliss Cotton DK (100% cotton – 92yd/84m per ball) in shade 42 plus 2 x ⅞oz (25g) balls of Madeira Nora (80% viscose/20% metallized polyester – 110yd/100m

per ball) in shade 328 (**E**)

1 x 3½oz (100g) hank of Blue Sky Alpacas Dyed Cotton (100% cotton – 150yd/137m per hank) in shade 607 (**F**)

1 x 3½oz (100g) ball of Patons 100% Cotton DK (100% cotton – 230yd/210m per ball) in shade 2719 (**I**)

Black and White Blocks

2 x 3½oz (100g) balls of Rowan Big Wool (100% merino – 87yd/80m per ball) in each of shades 01 (**A**) and 08 (**B**)

Page 62 Life's a Beach
Breaking Waves

A 15 x 3½oz (100g) hanks of Colinette Point 5 (100% wool – 54yd/50m per ball) in shade 142 Sea Breeze

B 3 x 3½oz (100g) balls of Rowan Big Wool (100% wool – 87yd/80m per ball) in shade 01 White

Surf's Up

3 x 3½oz (100g) balls of Rowan Big Wool (100% wool – 87yd/80m per ball) in shade 01 White

Page 66 Rustic Entrelac

A 9 x 3½oz (100g) hanks of Debbie Bliss Donegal Chunky Tweed (100% wool – 109yd/100m per ball) in shade 108

B 9 x 3½oz (100g) hanks of Debbie Bliss Donegal Chunky Tweed (100% wool – 109yd/100m per ball) in shade 112

Page 74 French Fancies
Taking the Floor

2 x 1¾oz (50g) balls of Jaeger Trinity (40% silk/35% cotton/25% polyamide fibre – 218yd/ 200m per ball) in shade 436

2 x 1¾oz (50g) balls of Rowan Wool Cotton (50% wool/50% cotton – 123yd/113m per ball) in shade 901

2 x 1¾oz (50g) balls of Rowan Handknit Cotton (100% cotton – 93yd/85m per ball) in shade 309

2 x 1¾oz (50g) balls of Rowan Classic Yarns Cashsoft DK (57% wool/33% microfibre/10% cashmere – 142yd/130m per ball) in shade 509

2 x 1¾oz (50g) balls of Debbie Bliss Rialto (100%

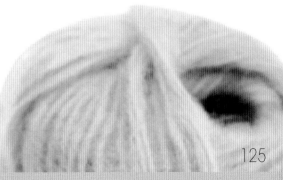

wool – 115yd/105m per ball) in shade 23009
2 x 1¾oz (50g) balls of Rowan Classic Yarns
Cashsoft DK (57% wool/33% microfibre/10%
cashmere – 142yd/130m per ball) in shade 501
2 x 1¾oz (50g) balls of Debbie Bliss Baby
Cashmerino (55% wool/33% microfibre/12%
cashmere – 136yd/125m per ball) in shade
340608
2 x 1¾oz (50g) balls of Debbie Bliss Baby
Cashmerino (55% wool/33% microfibre/12%
cashmere – 136yd/125m per ball) in shade
340010
2 x 1¾oz (50g) balls of Debbie Bliss Rialto (100%
wool – 115yd/105m per ball) in shade 23015
2 x 1¾oz (50g) balls of Patons Diploma Gold DK
(55% wool /25% acrylic/20% nylon – 131yd/120m
per ball) in shade 6245
2 x 1¾oz (50g) balls of Rowan Handknit Cotton
(100% cotton – 93yd/85m per ball) in shade 325

2 x 1¾oz (50g) balls of Patons Diploma Gold DK
(55% wool /25% acrylic/20% nylon – 131yd/120m
per ball) in shade 6222
2 x 1¾oz (50g) balls of Debbie Bliss Rialto (100%
wool – 115yd/105m per ball) in shade 23007

Flower Power
4 x 1¾oz (50g) balls of Jaeger Trinity (40%
silk/35% cotton/25% polyamide fibre – 218yd/
200m per ball) in shade 436
4 x 1¾oz (50g) balls of Rowan Wool Cotton
(50% wool/50% cotton – 123yd/113m per ball)
in shade 901
1 x 1¾oz (50g) balls of Rowan Classic Yarns
Cashsoft DK (57% wool/33% microfibre/10%
cashmere – 142yd/130m per ball) in shade 501
1 x 1¾oz (50g) balls of Debbie Bliss Baby
Cashmerino (55% wool/33% microfibre/12%
cashmere – 136yd/125m per ball) in shade
340010
1 x 1¾oz (50g) balls of Debbie Bliss Rialto (100%
wool – 115yd/105m per ball) in shade 23015
1 x 1¾oz (50g) balls of Debbie Bliss Rialto (100%
wool – 115yd/105m per ball) in shade 23007

Page 80 Denim Delight
11 x 1¾oz (50g) balls of Rowan Denim (100%
cotton – 102yd/93m per ball) in shade 229
9 x 1¾oz (50g) balls of Rowan Denim (100%
cotton – 102yd/93m per ball) in shade 231
4 x 1¾oz (50g) ball of Twilleys Denim Freedom
(100% cotton – 102yd/93m per ball) in shade 102
2 x 1¾oz (50g) ball of Twilleys Denim Freedom
(100% cotton – 102yd/93m per ball) in each of
shades 103 and 104
4 x 1¾oz (50g) ball of Twilleys Denim Freedom
(100% cotton – 102yd/93m per ball) in shade 102
5 x 1¾oz (50g) ball of Elle True Blue Denim (100%
cotton – 118yd/108m per ball) in shade 111
2 x 1¾oz (50g) ball of Elle True Blue Denim (100%
cotton – 118yd/108m per ball) in shade 112

Page 86 Romantic Roses
Rose Garden
A 19 x 1¾oz (50g) balls of Lang Silkdream (50%
merino/50% silk – 98yd/90m per ball) in shade 66
B 1 x 1¾oz (50g) ball of Rare Yarns Essentials
Cocoon Jade (70% merino/15% alpaca/7.5%
silk/7.5% mohair – 110yd/100m per ball) in Jade

Roses: 1 x 1¾oz (50g) ball of each of:
Sirdar Luxury Soft Cotton 4ply (100% cotton
– 225yd/208m per ball) in shade 661
Rowan 4ply Cotton (100% cotton – 186yd/170m
per ball) in shade 120

Patons Diploma Gold 4ply (55% wool/25%
acrylic/20% nylon – 201yd/184m per ball) in each
of shades 4294 and 4249
Patons Cotton 4ply (100% cotton – 361yd/330m
per ball) in shade 1701

Posy Pillowcase
A 6 x 1¾oz (50g) balls of Lang Silkdream (50%
merino/50% silk – 98yd/90m per ball) in shade 66
All other yarns same as Rose Garden

Page 92 Wobbly Stripe Seat
2 x 1¾oz (50g) balls of Rowan Big Wool (87yd/
80m per ball) in each of shades 29 (A) and 36 (D)
1 x 1¾oz (50g) ball of Rowan Big Wool (87yd/80m
per ball) in each of shades 25 (B) and 01 (C)

Page 96 Making Waves
Rippling Waves
A 7 x 1¾oz (50g) balls of Lang Silkdream (50%
merino/50% silk – 98yd/90m per ball) in shade 88
B 9 x 1¾oz (50g) balls of Lang Silkdream (50%
merino/50% silk – 98yd/90m per ball) in shade 72
C 9 x 1¾oz (50g) balls of Lang Silkdream (50%
merino/50% silk – 98yd/90m per ball) in shade 23
1 x 1¾oz (50g) ball of Debbie Bliss Baby
Cashmerino (55% merino/33% microfibre/12%
cashmere – 136yd/125m per ball) in each of
shades 002 (D), 202 (E) and 203 (G)
1 x 1¾oz (50g) ball of Debbie Bliss Cashmerino
DK (55% merino/33% microfibre/12% cashmere
– 120yd/110m per ball) in shade 20 (F)
1 x 1¾oz (50g) ball of Sirdar Baby Bamboo
(80% bamboo/20% wool – 104yd/95m per ball)
in shade 138 (H)
1 x 1¾oz (50g) ball of Rowan Handknit Cotton DK
(100% cotton – 93yd/85m per ball) in shade 316 (I)
1 x 1¾oz (50g) ball of Rowan Classics Cashcotton
4ply (35% cotton/25% polyamide/13%
viscose/9% cashmere – 197yd/180m per ball) in
shade 902 (J)

Wavy Wall Panel
A 2 x 1¾oz (50g) balls of Rowan Scottish
Tweed DK (100% wool – 123yd/113m per ball)
in shade 001
B 1 x 1¾oz (50g) balls of Rowan Classic Yarns Silk
Wool DK (50% merino/50% silk – 109yd/100m per
ball) in shade 305

suppliers

Contact the manufacturers for your local stockist or go to their websites for stockist and mail order information.

Art Yarns
www.artyarns.com
(US) 39 Westmoreland Avenue
White Plains, New York 10606
Tel: (914) 428 0333
(UK) Get Knitted
39 Brislington Hill, Brislington,
Bristol BS4 5BE
Tel: 0117 300 5211
www.getknitted.com
email: sales@getknitted.com

Blue Sky Alpacas
(US) Blue Sky Alpacas Inc
PO Box 88, Cedar, MN 55011
Tel: (763) 753 5815
www.blueskyalpacas.com
email: info@blueskyalpacas.com

Colinette
www.colinette.co.uk
(USA) Unique Kolours
28 North Bacton Hill Road
Malvern, PA 19355
Tel: (800) 252 3934
www.uniquekolours.com
(UK) Colinette Yarns Ltd
Banwy Workshops, Llanfair Caereinion
Powys, SY21 0SG
Tel: 01938 810128
email: feedback@colinette.com

Crystal Palace Yarns
(US) Crystal Palace Yarns
160 23rd St Richmond, CA 94804
Tel: (510) 237 9988
email: cpyinfo@straw.com
www.straw.com
(UK) Hantex Ltd
Whitehouse Yard, Eaudyke
Friskney, Boston, Lincolnshire, PE22 8NL
Tel: 01754 820800
www.hantex.co.uk
email: sales@hantex.co.uk

Debbie Bliss
www.debbieblissonline.com
(US) Knitting Fever Inc
315 Bayview Avenue, Amityville,
NY 11701
Tel: (516) 546 3600
www.knittingfever.com
email: admin@knittingfever.com
(UK) Designer Yarns Ltd,
Units 8–10 Newbridge Industrial Estate,
Pitt Street, Keighley
West Yorkshire, BD21 4PQ
Tel: 01535 664222
www.designeryarns.uk.com
email: enquiries@designeryarns.uk.com
(AUS) Prestige Yarns Pty Ltd
PO Box 39, Bulli, NSW 2516
Tel: +61 (0)2 4285 6669
www.prestigeyarns.com
email: info@prestigeyarns.com

GGH
www.ggh-garn.de
(USA) Muench Yarns Inc
1323 Scott Street, Petaluma
CA 94954-1135
Tel: (707) 763 9377
www.muenchyarns.com
email: info@muenchyarns.com
(UK) Designer Yarns Ltd,
Units 8–10 Newbridge Industrial Estate,
Pitt Street, Keighley
West Yorkshire, BD21 4PQ
Tel: 01535 664222
www.designeryarns.uk.com

Jaeger
(USA) Westminster Fibres Inc
4 Townsend West, Suite 8,
Nashua, NH 03063
Tel: (603) 886 5041
email: jaeger@westminsterfibers.com
(UK) Jaeger Handknits
Green Lane Mill, Holmfirth, HD9 2DX
Tel: 01484 680050
email: mail@knitrowan.com
(AUS) Australian Country Spinners
314–320 Albert Street,
Brunswick, Victoria 3056
Tel: 3 9380 3888
email: sales@auspinners.com.au

Kaalund
(US) Jumbuk Distribution
Tel: (949) 481 6696
email: donnaandaus@aol.com
(AUS) Kaalund Yarns Pty Ltd
PO Box 17, Banyo Qld 4014
Tel: +61 7 3267 6266
www.kaalundyarns.com.au
email: yarns@kaalundyarns.com.au
(UK) Auscraft
Tel: 01488 649 955
www.auscraft.co.uk
email: auscraft@auscraft.co.uk

Lang Yarns
www.langyarns.ch
(USA) Berroco Inc
PO Box 367, 14 Elmdale Road
US-01569 Uxbridge
MA 01569
Tel: (508) 278 2527
www.berroco.com
email: info@berroco.com
(UK) Artyarn
Tel: 01526 832095
www.artyarn.co.uk
email: info@artyarn.co.uk

Louisa Harding
www.louisaharding.co.uk
(USA) Knitting Fever Inc
KFI-Roosevelt, NY 11574
Tel: (516) 546 3600
www.knittingfever.com

(UK) Designer Yarns Ltd
Units 8–10 Newbridge Industrial Estate,
Pitt Street, Keighley,
West Yorkshire, BD21 4PQ
Tel: 01535 664222
www.designeryarns.uk.com
email: enquiries@designeryarns.uk.com

Noro
(USA) Knitting Fever Inc
KFI-Roosevelt, NY 11574
Tel: (516) 546 3600
www.knittingfever.com
(UK) Designer Yarns Ltd
Units 8–10 Newbridge Industrial Estate,
Pitt Street, Keighley,
West Yorkshire, BD21 4PQ
Tel: 01535 664222
www.designeryarns.uk.com
email: enquiries@designeryarns.uk.com
(AUS) Prestige Yarns Pty Ltd
PO Box 39, Bulli, NSW 2516
Tel: +61 02 4285 6669
www.prestigeyarns.com
email: info@prestigeyarns.com

Patons
(USA) 320 Livingstone Avenue South,
Listowel, ON, Canada N4W 3H3
Tel: 1-888-368-8401
www.patonsyarns.com
email: inquire@spinriteyarns.com
(UK) Coats Craft UK
PO Box 22, Lingfield House
Lingfield Point, McMullen Road
Darlington , DL1 1YQ
Tel: 01325 394394
www.coatscrafts.co.uk
email: consumer.ccuk@coats.com
(AUS) 314 Albert Street
Brunswick, Victoria 3056
Tel: +61 3 9380 3888
www.patons.biz
email: enquiries@auspinners.com.au

Rare Yarns
www.rareyarns.com.au
(UK) Spin a Yarn
3 Station Road, Bovey Tracey,
Devon, TQ13 9AL
Tel: 01626 836203
www.spinayarndevon.co.uk
email: info@spinayarndevon.co.uk
(AUS & NZ) The Rare Yarns Company in
New Zealand
The Grape Escape Complex, McShanes
Road, RD1 Richmond, Nelson
Tel: +64 3 544 0063
email: info@rareyarns.com.au

Rowan
www.knitrowan.com
(USA) Rowan USA, 4 Townsend West
Suite 8, Nashua, NH 03063
Tel: (603) 886 5041
email: rowan@westminsterfibers.com

(UK) Rowan
Green Lane Mill, Holmfirth, HD9 2DX
Tel: 01484 681881
email: mail@knitrowan.com
(AUS) Australian Country Spinners
314–320 Albert Street, Brunswick, Victoria
3056
Tel: 3 9380 3888
email: sales@auspinners.com.au

Rowan Classic Yarns
www.ryclassic.com
(USA) Westminster Fibres Inc
4 Townsend West, Suite 8, Nashua,
NH 03063
Tel: (603) 886 5041
email: ryc@westminsterfibers.com
(UK) RYC
Green Lane Mill, Holmfirth, HD9 2BR
Tel: 01484 681881
email: mail@ryclassic.com
(AUS) Australian Country Spinners
314–320 Albert Street, Brunswick,
Victoria 3056
Tel: 3 9380 3888
email: sales@auspinners.com.au

Sirdar
www.sirdar.co.uk
(USA) Knitting Fever Inc.
KFI-Roosevelt, NY 11574
Tel: 516 546 3600
www.knittingfever.com
(UK) Sirdar Spinning Ltd
Flanshaw Lane, Alverthorpe,
Wakefield, WF2 9ND
Tel: 01924 371501
email: enquiries@sirdar.co.uk
(AUS) Creative Images
PO Box 106, Hastings, Victoria 3915
Tel: 03 5979 1555
email: creative@peninsula.starway.net.au

Trendsetter Yarns
(US) Trendsetter Yarns
16745 Saticoy Street #101
Van Nuys, CA 91406
Tel: (818) 780 5497
www.trendsetteryarns.com
email:info@trendsetteryarns.com
(UK) Bloomsbury Trading Company
Tel: 01665 606062
www.bloomsburytrading.co.uk

Twilleys
www.twilleys.co.uk
(UK) Twilleys of Stamford
Roman Mill, Stamford, PE9 1BG
Tel: 01780 752661
email: twilleys@tbramsden.co.uk

about the author

Claire Crompton has worked in the knitting industry for almost 20 years. After a Knitwear Design degree she became a pattern designer for major yarn manufacturers such as Sirdar and DMC. She is the author of *The Knitter's Bible*, *The Knitter's Bible: Knitted Accessories* and *The Knitter's Bible: Knitted Bags*. She lives in Gunnislake, Cornwall. See Claire's website for more information: **www.clairecrompton.co.uk**.

acknowledgments

I would like to thank Heather Hess at Auscraft and Kaalund Yarns, Australia, for generously supplying the materials for the Floral Fantasy cushion (page 25). Thanks also to Lorna Yabsley for the fantastic photography and to the models.

At David & Charles, thanks go to Jennifer Fox-Proverbs, Bethany Dymond, Sarah Underhill, Charly Bailey and Emma Sandquest for creating this book. Finally, thanks to Nicola Hodgson for editing once again.

index